ALICE IN WONDERLAND
AND
PHILOSOPHY

The Blackwell Philosophy and Pop Culture Series
Series Editor: William Irwin

ALICE IN WONDERLAND
AND
PHILOSOPHY

CURIOUSER AND CURIOUSER

Edited by Richard Brian Davis

WILEY

John Wiley & Sons, Inc.

Published by John Wiley & Sons, Inc., Hoboken, New Jersey
Published simultaneously in Canada

Chapter opener design by Forty-Five Degree Design LLC

For general information about our other products and services, please contact our Customer Care Department within the United States at (800) 762-2974, outside the United States at (317) 572-3993 or fax (317) 572-4002.

Wiley also publishes its books in a variety of electronic formats. Some content that appears in print may not be available in electronic books. For more information about Wiley products, visit our web site at www.wiley.com.

Library of Congress Cataloging-in-Publication Data:

Alice in Wonderland and Philosophy : curiouser and curiouser / edited by Richard Brian Davis.
p. cm.
Includes bibliographical references and index.
ISBN 978-0-470-55836-2 (pbk.)
1. Carroll, Lewis, 1832-1898. Alice's adventures in Wonderland. 2. Philosophy in literature. 3. Literature–Philosophy. I. Davis, Richard Brian, 1963–
PR4611.A73A54 2010
823' .8–dc22

2009037590

Printed in the United States of America

10 9 8 7 6 5 4 3

CONTENTS

PART FOUR
"WHO IN THE WORLD AM I?"

ACKNOWLEDGMENTS

"It's My Own Invention"–Yeah, Right!

"Oh, I've had such a curious dream." Since it seems as though I've just edited a book, I'd better single out a few individuals for special praise. Thanks are due to Connie Santisteban at Wiley, who was no doubt tempted (at points) to speak the dreaded words of the White Rabbit: "Oh my ears and whiskers, how late it's getting!" She didn't. And to Bill Irwin, who pushed me—or rather let me jump—into the rabbit hole. Working with Bill is sweet: "a sort of mixed flavour of cherry-tart, custard, pineapple, roast turkey, toffee, and hot buttered toast." And finally, to my daughters, Madelyn and Emma, who urged me on at every turn. My wish for you is that you would grow up to be (in Megan Lloyd's words) as "unflappable, confident, assertive" as Alice herself. To Madelyn and Emma Davis, I dedicate this book.

INTRODUCTION
You're Late for a Very Important Date

"You take the blue pill," Morpheus says to Neo in *The Matrix*, "and the story ends. . . . You take the red pill and you stay in Wonderland, and I show you how deep the rabbit-hole goes." It's a tempting offer, isn't it? For at one time or another in our lives, we've all wanted to *escape*—from a dull and tedious job, an impossible relationship, from a world in which we often have so little control over what happens to us. Perhaps it's for reasons such as these that our culture has become positively obsessed with the idea of transcending the confines of this world for the cool fresh air of another. Whether it's by a red pill, a secret wardrobe, a looking glass, or a rabbit-hole, it doesn't really matter. We'll take it.

Of course, we don't just want to know how *deep* the rabbit-hole goes. That's a given; after all, it's a portal to another world—"four thousand miles down, I think." We also want to know how to make sense of what we *discover* when we suddenly land "thump! thump!" in Wonderland and pass through the looking glass. And Alice's Wonderland is an oh! so curious place filled with both dangers and delights. Here we encounter blue caterpillars who smoke hookahs, babies who turn into pigs, cats whose grins remain after their heads have faded away, and a Mad Hatter who speaks to Time. There is a White Queen who lives backward and remembers forward, and there are trials in which the sentence is handed down first with the evidence and verdict given out only afterward. And you'd better be on your best behavior while there. As the Red Queen sees it, beheading is a punishment that fits *every* crime!

We've spoken of Wonderland's dangers, but what of its delights? Why should anyone *want* to travel to such a world? As Cheshire Puss tells Alice, you must be mad "or you wouldn't have come here." Is Wonderland simply a land of sheer nonsense, or is there a method to Lewis Carroll's madness? Well, as the Duchess wisely observes, "Everything's got a moral, if only you can find it." And the moral of the book you now hold in your hands is that there are deep philosophical riches to be had in *Alice's Adventures in Wonderland* and *Through the Looking-Glass*, answers to life's ultimate questions, if only you have the proper guide.

You don't have to be blue, a caterpillar, or under the effects of the hookah to ask a deep question like "Who in the world am I?" As Alice says, "*That's* the great puzzle!" Indeed it is. How can I know whether this or that job is right for *me*, if I don't know who me *is*? Indeed, how can I know what I can become in the future? (Hardly any of us, I dare say, is satisfied with who we are at present.) And to know the answers to these questions, I must know who I *have been*. I must remember. But that's often my problem: I forget. What to do? What to do? The Alice-addicted philosophers in this book will clear the air of the hookah smoke and forward you the decryption codes for unlocking your personal identity. And you'll be glad they did.

As you read on, you'll be amazed to discover why nice girls don't make history (and Alice is better than any Disney princess); what the Red Queen can teach us about nuclear strategy; whether we should do more with mushrooms than just eat them (and what sort of "trip" to expect if we do); and how Alice, procrastination, and the Spice Girls are all mysteriously connected. "What a curious feeling!" You can put it all together for the first time. So "Read Me." Venture to taste this book, and if "finding it very nice," we recommend that you "very soon finish it off."

PART ONE

"WAKE UP, ALICE DEAR"

UNRULY ALICE: A FEMINIST VIEW OF SOME ADVENTURES IN WONDERLAND

Megan S. Lloyd

"Come to class ready to discuss and defend your favorite fairy-tale heroine," I told my students in "Unruly Women through the Ages." The course began as a survey of feminist archetypes and issues, but it quickly became a forum for a group of rather unruly female students aged eighteen to twenty-two to discuss candidly topics such as date rape, abortion, sexual harassment, battered women, male and female relationships, anorexia and bulimia, and what it means to be a woman today. For one class period, we turned to the realm of fairy tales. To my initial question, I expected students to write about Little Red Riding Hood or Goldilocks, but most students chose a Disney princess—Cinderella, Ariel, Belle, Mulan, mostly unruly females going against the flow of male rules imposed upon them. Two students, however, chose Alice as their favorite unruly fairy tale character. They argued that

Alice, unlike other fairy-tale heroines, requires no fairy god-mother, huntsman, or good fairy—just her own wits and ingenuity—to navigate through Wonderland successfully, keeping her head intact. My students know Alice not through Carroll but through Disney, and this Disney heroine Alice is a precursor to the strong Belle and Mulan and counter to the pliable Cinderella and the passive Aurora and Snow White, who require male aid to bring them to life and reality again.

In Carroll's or Disney's version, Alice's journey through Wonderland has long been seen as a tale of identity, agency, and adulthood. The curiosity and confidence that Carroll instills in Alice connect her with other unruly women we studied in class, such as Lysistrata, Shakespeare's Kate, Emma Bovary, Marie Antoinette, Marilyn Monroe, Hillary Clinton, Sarah Palin, Camille Paglia, Pandora, and Eve. Alice's direct, candid approach to life is refreshing and something the young women in my class can relate to. They understand the story of a young woman who has the world before her, ready to embark on life, who changes herself, primarily by eating and drinking, to fit in. She encounters all types, tests herself, tastes life around her, and once she learns the right combination to fit in and be comfortable with herself, she's welcomed into a beautiful world where she possesses wisdom, power, and prestige.[1]

Nice Girls Don't Make History

As if by instinct, Alice follows the White Rabbit down the hole "never once considering how in the world she was to get out again."[2] Landing, she feels no fear, but rather engages in her surroundings and wonders how far she has fallen. "At such a fall as this, I shall think nothing of tumbling downstairs!"[3] This self-assurance and unquestioning spirit, this Pandora mentality or, as some would say reckless, wild, impetuous streak, is also the kind of indomitable spirit today's young women appreciate.

Alice rejects and frees herself from stereotypical female traits; she is not trapped by the confines of roles or requirements. First, she rejects the world her sister occupies; then in her journey through Wonderland she questions the nurturing role of mother; and finally she stands up to seemingly powerful females and males alike, including the Queen of Hearts, the Caterpillar, the Mad Hatter, and the Cheshire Cat. Alice's confident attitude leads her safely through Wonderland and she begins "to think that very few things indeed were really impossible," a message young women of today need to keep in mind.[4] Plucky, undaunted, and impervious to the dangers that may lie in Wonderland, Alice is a curious, empowered seven-year-old girl eager to delve into a new world she chooses to enter. What a wonderful model for our young women to look up to!

Alice's intrepid attitude elicits some criticism, however. In Carroll's original and Disney's rendition, Alice may seem abrasive. As my students came to realize in our historical survey, society all too often ridicules strong women, interpreting assertive actions as aggressive and transgressive. The powerful, autonomous woman to some may be the impetuous, reckless, and unruly woman to others. Indeed, Alice eats and drinks what she sees, intrudes, barges in, takes her seat at the tea party uninvited, hears a squeaking pencil from one juror and takes it from him,[5] uses her intellect to solve problems, and frequently speaks her mind—everything young women should do. Nice girls don't make history, after all. Alice is assertive, and unfortunately, almost 150 years after Carroll's publication, in Wonderland and today that assertiveness can still seem pushy, forward, and aggressive.

Alice is not like the other females in Carroll's stories, and this contrast appeals to my students and makes Alice an important female advocate. Even before she enters Wonderland, Alice has begun to reject the female reality her sister has chosen, a passive compliance, fulfilling a traditional female role. Her sister presents one vision of women, those well educated with little to do. Reading a book "without pictures or conversations" is of no use to Alice, and she seeks other means to occupy herself.[6] Next she contemplates making a daisy chain but wonders "whether the pleasure of making a daisy chain would be worth the trouble of getting up and picking the daises."[7] Significantly, the White Rabbit appears as Alice questions this busywork that would garner no productive results. Neither sitting and reading nor making daisy chains, Alice follows the White Rabbit down the hole and thus chooses an active function within the world, even if that world is Wonderland.

Motherhood Is Not a Requirement

Alice's journey in Wonderland begins with a rejection of one female stereotype, the idle woman, embodied in her sister reading to while away the time. Continuing her journey in Wonderland, Alice learns more about the power of women when she literally opens the door for herself. In chapter VI, "Pig and Pepper," Alice finds herself at the Duchess's door and knocks, but to no avail. This exchange between Alice and the Frog-Footman follows:

> "But what am *I* to do?" said Alice.
> "Anything you like," said the Footman, and began whistling.
> "Oh, there's no use in talking to him," said Alice desperately: "he's perfectly idiotic!" And she opened the door and went in.[8]

Her inability to enter the house through conventional means, acting the proper, demure female, causes Alice to question her situation: "What am *I* to do?" The Frog-Footman's response, "Anything you like," opens up all possibilities for her. Here she learns that the norms of society that she may follow really mean very little. She has the power to do anything within herself, a theme that recurs throughout Carroll's works. Alice's message for today—in Wonderland and the world at large—is that young women can do anything they like.

The world of possibility for women that Wonderland offers Alice includes an indifferent perspective toward motherhood, which in Victorian England (and in some places still today) was the primary function of women. Alice views the pride and pitfalls of maternity with a great deal of detachment. The Pigeon presents Alice with her first look at motherhood, a mother who expresses the suffering that comes with that role. Their meeting begins with the Pigeon beating a long-necked Alice.

"Serpent!" screamed the Pigeon.

"I'm *not* a serpent!" said Alice indignantly. "Let me alone!"

"Serpent, I say again!" repeated the Pigeon, but in a more subdued tone, and added, with a kind of sob, "I've tried every way, but nothing seems to suit them! . . .

"I've tried the roots of trees, and I've tried banks, and I've tried hedges," the Pigeon went on, without attending to her; "but those serpents! There's no pleasing them! . . .

"As if it wasn't trouble enough hatching the eggs," said the Pigeon; but I must be on the look-out for serpents, night and day! Why, I haven't had a wink of sleep these three weeks!"

"I'm very sorry you've been annoyed," said Alice, who was beginning to see its meaning.

"And just as I'd taken the highest tree in the wood," continued the Pigeon, raising its voice to a shriek, "and just as I was thinking I should be free of them at last, they must needs come wriggling down from the sky! Ugh, Serpent!"

"But I'm *not* a serpent, I tell you!" said Alice. "I'm a—I'm a— . . .

> "I—I'm a little girl," said Alice rather doubtfully, as she remembered the number of changes she had gone through that day.
>
> "A likely story indeed!" said the Pigeon in a tone of the deepest contempt. "I've seen a good many little girls in my time, but never *one* with such a neck as that! No, no! You're a serpent; and there's no use denying it. I suppose you'll be telling me next that you never tasted an egg!"
>
> "I *have* tasted eggs, certainly," said Alice, who was a very truthful child; "but little girls eat eggs quite as much as serpents do, you know. . . .
>
> "I'm not looking for eggs, as it happens; and, if I was, I shouldn't want *yours*."[9]

In this exchange, Alice fails to commiserate with the Pigeon's state as the maternally inclined might do, but instead apologizes for annoying her. Alice's line, "little girls eat eggs quite as much as serpents do," even resonates with today's pro-life/pro-choice discussion. The Pigeon names long-necked Alice a serpent; not rejecting this role for the Pigeon's maternal one, Alice aligns herself with the serpent, predator to pigeons and eggs; rejects maternity, at least for the time being; and claims her autonomy.

Alice next encounters the maternal life of the Duchess. The ugly Duchess nurses a howling baby in a smoky kitchen. To contemporary readers, Carroll's Duchess figures as a stereotypical white-trash mother, one who screams at her child, fails to consider its well-being (in a smoke-filled room with flying debris just missing it), and accompanies her sadistic song not with soothing rocks but severe shakes at every line. Tired of her crying child, the Duchess finally flings the baby at Alice and departs to do something better, like "play croquet with the Queen."[10] Today, this Duchess could be arrested for shaken baby syndrome or be demonized, like Britney Spears and Casey Anthony, and plastered all over the media.[11] Alice, herself, sees how unfit for motherhood the Duchess is, remarking, "If I don't take this child away with me . . . they're sure to kill it in a day or two."[12] Alice's disregard for the Duchess surfaces again when she learns that the Duchess, a prisoner of the Queen, is to be executed.

"What for?" said Alice.

"Did you say 'What a pity!'?" the Rabbit asked.

"No, I didn't," said Alice. "I don't think it's at all a pity."[13]

Alice catches the Duchess's strange child, which ultimately transforms into a pig, and her indifferent treatment of it offers another view of motherhood. No cooing, tickling, or speaking baby talk; she first chastises the child, saying, "Don't grunt, . . . that's not at all a proper way of expressing yourself."[14] Unlike so many stereotypical women, Alice does not exhibit "cute baby syndrome," seeing any infant as darling, no matter how ugly, simply because it's small. Indeed, "Alice did not like the look of the thing at all."[15]

"If you're going to turn into a pig, my dear," said Alice, seriously, "I'll have nothing more to do with you. Mind now!" . . .

Alice was just beginning to think to herself, "Now, what am I to do with this creature, when I get it home?" when it grunted again, so violently, that she looked down into its face in some alarm. This time there could be *no* mistake about it: it was neither more nor less than a pig, and she felt that it would be quite absurd for her to carry it any further.

So she set the little creature down, and felt quite relieved to see it trot away quietly into the wood.[16]

While I might not hire Alice as a baby-sitter or pet-sitter, I'm happy to see a young woman honestly show her attitude toward children. Not sympathetic to the Pigeon's complaints nor surprised that the Duchess is imprisoned, Alice exhibits a rational, contemporary view of motherhood, a view my students share. For them, and perhaps for Carroll, motherhood is not a requirement for worth.

What Would Alice Do?

Alice's independent spirit takes her to the all-male world of the Mad Hatter's tea party. "No room," they all cry when they see her coming. But this doesn't sway her a bit. "There's *plenty* of room!" she declares "indignantly."[17] The Mad Hatter's tea party presents an assertive female in a male world. She gets stuck at a very messy table (like frat brothers, March Hare, Dormouse, and Mad Hatter prefer to move to the next spot rather than do any washing up), and Alice eventually understands that while she's free to join them, she's not obliged to be a part of their world.

The exchange between Alice and the guests at the Mad Hatter's tea party is particularly abrasive and shows us how Alice has grown (not just physically) in her journey through Wonderland. Here she speaks more freely, asks questions, objects to what someone says, challenges rude remarks, and attempts to engage in the wordplay between the Mad Hatter, the Dormouse, and March Hare. She wants to keep up with the boys, and indeed she succeeds in this male world of teacups and chatter. However, a direct threat to her very intellect forces her to leave. After the Dormouse's story, this exchange takes place:

> "Really, now you ask me," said Alice, very much confused, "I don't think—"
> "Then you shouldn't talk," said the Hatter.
> This piece of rudeness was more than Alice could bear: she got up in great disgust, and walked off.[18]

The Mad Hatter's glib remark sounds all too familiar as women, even contemporary ones, try to advance in the workplace. The Mad Hatter requires quick thinking but fails to see the intellect in a seven-year-old who has used her own wits to make it this far into Wonderland. The misogynist Mad Hatter disrespects methodical and contemplative Alice and, like his cohorts, couldn't care less when she departs: "the Dormouse fell asleep instantly, and neither of the others took the least notice of her going."[19] Although Alice, the new young woman in this old-boy network, doesn't put up with their harassment, she leaves, "look[ing] back once or twice, half hoping that they would call after her"[20]; thus she may want to be part of their world, as she looks back with some remorse. However, her decision to depart this chauvinistic space gains her the garden she has sought from her first arrival in Wonderland, and with it comes respect. Once in the garden, Alice is honored for who she is; the cards bow low before her.[21]

Another affront to Alice's intellect comes from a female who wants Alice to display stereotypically passive female traits. In contrast to the sexist Mad Hatter, who requires women to think in his presence but doesn't give them a chance, Carroll presents the other extreme, the Duchess, who wants Alice to take a "dumb blonde" approach to life. Thanks to Alice, the Duchess has been summoned out of jail to discuss the Cheshire Cat. Alice is surprised to find the Duchess in a good mood, which she attributes to the pepper in her kitchen;[22] however, the absence of a child and thus the Duchess's child care duties may be the real reason for a change in her disposition. Even without a child, the Duchess still irritates Alice, first physically and then intellectually. A number of times Alice notes how "*very* ugly" she is[23]; she's also the right size to rest her chin on Alice's shoulder, digging into it uncomfortably. The Duchess walks with Alice spewing morals for everything, actually mindless clichés to fill the time, digging her chin into Alice's shoulder all the while. On two occasions, the Duchess questions Alice's thought. "You're thinking about something, my dear, and that makes you forget to talk," says the Duchess, reinforcing the stereotype of the talkative woman and encouraging Alice to conform.[24]

> "Thinking again?" the Duchess asked, with another dig of her sharp little chin.
>
> "I've a right to think," said Alice sharply, for she was beginning to feel a little worried.
>
> "Just about as much right," said the Duchess, "as pigs have to fly."[25]

Digging her chin into Alice's shoulder, the Duchess underscores this infuriating verbal reprimand, shared by all too many even today. Like the Mad Hatter before her, the Duchess attempts to put Alice in her place, but throughout Wonderland, Alice alters, changes, and acts to satisfy herself.

Alice displays her intellect in one final growth spurt when she is asked to testify at the Knave's trial. Here she speaks her mind to the figure in power, the King, not the Queen, who orders her out of the court according to "Rule Forty-two—*All persons more than a mile high to leave the court.*"[26] She astutely challenges this rule, remains to hear more evidence, and finally calls the court what it is: "You're nothing but a pack of cards!"[27] Her defiance at the tea party provides her access to the garden; this defiant move transports her to reality. A curious, inquisitive girl at the beginning of her journey in Wonderland, by this time she has grown larger again and regains her full size. Her physical growth mirrors her social, psychological, and emotional development. Alice has become a large, powerful presence, a fully realized young woman who is ready to challenge anyone, especially those who obfuscate the truth. In fact, the truth sets her free and wakens her into reality once again.

Unflappable, confident, assertive, no Cinderella complex here: Alice is not simply a little Victorian girl having an adventure; she is a model for the twenty-first-century woman. Alice bravely enters into a new world and takes care of herself. Who wouldn't want a self-confident figure like Alice to look up to?

Alice's sister attempts to escape through reading and daydreaming, but unlike Alice, who plunges down the rabbit-hole in pursuit, her sister falls into a female trap, accepting what's in front of her and not fully understanding the agency and opportunity within herself. "[S]he sat on, with closed eyes, and half believed herself in Wonderland, though she knew she had but to open them again, and all would change to dull reality."[28] Her sister dreams, but she is stuck enduring a reality that Alice, we hope, will not accept. By rejecting daisy chains and following white rabbits, assertive Alice already sees the possibility in the real world she occupies. Alice offers another world for young women, one that need not be dull. Hers is a reality where women author their own tales, work out their own problems, expect the extraordinary, and speak their minds. Faced with continuing mistreatment and stereotypical expectations, today's young women do well to ask themselves, what would Alice do?

NOTES

1. Judith Little talks about feminist Alice and other literary heroines in "Liberated Alice: Dodgson's Female Hero as Domestic Rebel," *Women's Studies* 3 (1976): 195–205.
2. Lewis Carroll, *The Annotated Alice: The Definitive Edition*, ed. Martin Gardner (New York: W.W. Norton, 2000), 12. All subsequent references to *Alice's Adventures in Wonderland* come from this text.
3. Ibid., 13.
4. Ibid., 16.
5. Ibid., 111–112.
6. Ibid., 11.
7. Ibid.
8. Ibid., 59–60.
9. Ibid., 54–56.
10. Ibid., 62.
11. Casey Anthony is the mother accused of the murder of her two-year-old daughter, Caylee.
12. Carroll, *The Annotated Alice*, 63.
13. Ibid., 84.

14. Ibid., 63.
15. Ibid.
16. Ibid., 63–64.
17. Ibid., 69.
18. Ibid., 77.
19. Ibid.
20. Ibid.
21. Ibid., 80.
22. Ibid., 90.
23. Ibid., 91.
24. Ibid.
25. Ibid., 93.
26. Ibid., 120.
27. Ibid., 124.
28. Ibid., 126.

JAM YESTERDAY, JAM TOMORROW, BUT NEVER JAM TODAY: ON PROCRASTINATION, HIKING, AND . . . THE SPICE GIRLS?

Mark D. White

Do you enjoy your job? Many people say they do, but what exactly do they mean? I'd guess that they mean they like their jobs in general, or in broad view, as they fit in with the rest of their lives and goals. They may have good memories of their time in a job, perhaps anticipating progress, promotion, and prosperity in times to come. But if you asked them if they like the day-to-day experience of their job, they might sing a different tune, most likely in a distinctly minor key. Now you would hear a tune of drudgery and woe, wailing of the monotony of endless meetings and mountains of e-mail, interrupted only by spells of stale coffee and watercooler blather.

But how can this be? How can many days of doldrums add up to a career of sunshine and bunny rabbits? Let's ask Alice, who had a similar experience when the White Queen offered her a job. Her tale may shed some light on things like jobs, parenting, and exercise, and even offer some insights into procrastination, which—appropriately enough—we'll get to later (if at all).

Never Jam Today?

In *Through the Looking-Glass*, the White Queen offers Alice a job as her "lady's-maid," with a compensation package of "twopence a week, and jam every other day." Alice protests that she doesn't care for jam, and in any case doesn't want any jam today. The Queen clarifies, "You couldn't have it if you *did* want it. The rule is, jam to-morrow and jam yesterday—but never jam *to-day*." Alice, of course, is puzzled by this (though apparently not at the prospect of the job offer itself), arguing that "it *must* come sometimes to 'jam to-day.'"[1]

Can we make sense of this sticky situation? Must it, in fact, come sometimes to "jam to-day"? As it happens—and I wouldn't mention it if it didn't, you know, so it must have happened so—the contemporary philosopher Elijah Millgram, inspired by our dear Alice, has written about such "jam-yesterday-jam-tomorrow" goods.[2] In his view, the example from the introduction—no, don't go back and reread it, or you'll never get to what follows—would be a jam-yesterday-jam-tomorrow good. When our proud worker looks back over her past experience of the job, she remembers good times; when she looks forward into the future (it's right over that hill, behind those trees), she also sees nothing but happiness and mirth. Jam yesterday, and jam tomorrow—but is there jam today? Heavens, no—in the vernacular of our times, for the worker of our tale, today sucks. (She's not reading this book, obviously—aren't you glad you are, then?) There is no jam today for our toiling laborer, nor any other day in which she finds herself.

Millgram argues that many experiences in life appear like this to us: very good when we remember or anticipate them, but quite ordinary or downright bad in the moment. He mentions parenting, which most people—even *your* parents, I would wager, if I were a betting person, which I'm not—will cite as a marvelous, transcendent life adventure. They may be looking back in old age on their attempts at steering their spawn toward social responsibility and a fine career in the fast food industry, or looking forward in their youth to a life filled with unconditional love, warm hugs that never stop, and free French fries. But most of the day-to-day tasks of childrearing are mundane at best, disgusting at worst: changing diapers, wiping up spills, shuttling little ones from activity to activity, and bailing them out of jail.

Another example Millgram gives is hiking. (Mind you, he teaches in Utah—they hike a lot there.) Hiking enthusiasts—that is, Utah residents—look forward to the day's hike, and after they're done they look back on the experience fondly, but at any given moment during the hike they're usually sweaty, their feet hurt, or they realize, "Wow, I'm hiking—I must be in Utah." Once again, jam yesterday, jam tomorrow, but no jam today. But how can a series of moments, none of them particularly pleasant, tally up to an experience that you recall later as wonderful and that you anticipate as exhilarating? And does it have anything to do with Utah?

The Organic Unity of "Wannabe"

Let's travel across the pond—can't hike there, alas—from Millgram's Utah to Alice's England, where once there lived a philosopher by the name of G. E. Moore (1873–1958).[3] Moore is perhaps best known for describing the *naturalistic fallacy*, by which he meant that natural properties cannot imply moral goodness (which should settle the whole hiking issue once and for all, I think).[4] But the idea of Moore's that we are more

interested in here is what he called *organic unity*, which has
nothing to do with overpriced vegetables and hemp shirts, but
rather with how the value of a "whole" relates to the separate
values of the parts that make it up.[5]

There is a common saying—why, I was just saying it
the other day, and I am very common indeed—that goes, "the
whole is greater than the sum of its parts." Just think of any
great rock group—the Beatles, Led Zeppelin, the Spice Girls,
take your pick—and even as good as the individual members
of those bands may be, something special was created when
they recorded and performed together. The four lads from
Liverpool certainly created some fantastic music on their own
after the band broke up, but few would say any of it compares
to the collective output. Same with Zeppelin, Kiss, the Rolling
Stones—and certainly none of the Girls have come up with a
"Wannabe" on their own, have they?

While he didn't use the "Wannabe" argument—at least
not in his published work, although a Union Jack leotard is
rumored to have been found among his effects—Moore gen-
eralized this sentiment, writing that "the value of a whole must
not be assumed to be the same as the sum of the values of its
parts,"[6] and describing such a whole as an "organic unity."[7]
By this he means that the whole has a value all its own in virtue
of being a distinct thing in and of itself, a value that cannot
be found in the value of its parts. The vocal talents of Robert
Plant certainly have value, as do the musical skills of Jimmy
Page, John Paul Jones, and John Bonham, but Led Zeppelin
as a band had value that transcends the collective value of its
members. There is a value created by the four of them col-
laborating in the studio or onstage that simply does not exist
when they each play separately, and this is what Moore was on
about.[8]

This is all well and good—but what if not all the parts of a
whole are well or good? What if some parts are good and some
are rather poor, or downright bad? Moore considers this: "It is

certain that a whole formed of a good thing and an indifferent thing may have immensely greater value than that good thing itself possesses. And it seems as if indifferent things may also be the sole constituents of a whole which has great value, either positive or negative."[9] Think about Wham!—just when you thought I couldn't sink any lower. Though having no apparent value of his own, Andrew Ridgely did contribute to the early success of George Michael. And even though none of the members of U2 on his own could possibly make a living delivering singing telegrams to the dead, the four of them together produce music that (implausible as it may sound—literally!) appeals to some people with breath still in their bodies.

Moore cannot even rule out the possibility that "the addition of a bad thing to a good whole may increase the positive value of the whole, or the addition of a bad thing to a bad may produce a whole having positive value," though he considers them both to be "doubtful."[10] This makes some sense—you don't add a lame singer to a band to make the band *better* (are you listening, INXS?). And you certainly don't get a good band out of four bad musicians—after all, even the guys in U2 aren't *bad* musicians, so together they can have some sort of magic. But all the same, adding a fifth member to a four-piece band, even if she's not the greatest, can "complete" the group—I mean, seriously, could Posh Spice even *sing*? But you can't imagine the Spice Girls without her, can you? (Go on, try . . . told you so.)[11]

More Millgram, Less Moore

So let's jet back to Utah and rejoin our good friend Elijah Millgram and the jam-yesterday-jam-tomorrow idea regarding everyday experiences. How does this connect with Moore? Recall that such goods are only seen as good in remembrance or anticipation, but never during the actual experience of them. The problem, then, becomes this: how can a number of momentary experiences, none of which are considered good at the time, add up to an overall experience that is either remembered as good, or anticipated as good? The experiences are the parts, and the memory or anticipation is of the whole—so there *is* Moore to Millgram than meets the eye after all!

Certainly, a life experience like parenting or work can be considered an organic unity—a whole whose value is not necessarily equal to the summed-up value of its parts. This would be easy to accept if all of the parts—the momentary experiences—were at least indifferent, and some of them rather good, if not amazing. Suppose I spend a year overseas tending to the ill (as I am wont to do from time to time—when Time comes, of course, and he hasn't yet), and I am later asked about the overall experience. If each day were at least pleasant (reading to the blind, say), but there were enough fantastic days (restoring sight to the blind), then I could reasonably conclude that the year I spent—utterly selflessly, I agree, though I don't like to mention it—was a good one. It would still be reasonable to say that even if there were an occasional bad day (I could not find any more people who needed my help because I had simply done *that* much good), for very few real-world experiences lasting any decent length of time are without moments of misery and woe. (Just think of the films of Keanu Reeves—utterly brilliant overall, but with all-too-frequent woe.)

But in the most extreme version we are discussing, people who "enjoy" jam-yesterday-jam-tomorrow goods *never* have jam today. If I traveled overseas and was never successful in helping anybody, but I later reported that "I had a wonderful time, wish you'd have been there," you'd either think me insincere or insane (but sincerely so). My answer would seem even more absurd—maybe even Spice Girls absurd—if perhaps I fell ill myself while there, making some days (even everyday) profoundly miserable. But Millgram argues, in the complete absence of absurdity, that long-term experiences like parenting and work can often be exactly like this, full of mundane or even bad momentary experiences, but described in retrospect or prospect as good overall.

Can Moore help us here? Near the end of *Principia Ethica*, he makes a very subtle distinction (as philosophers often do—remind me to tell you about *intentionality* and *intensionality* someday, if you ever need drying off) between "the value which a thing possesses '*as a whole*,' and that which it possesses '*on the whole*.'"[12] The value of a thing "on the whole" refers to its overall value, while its value "as a whole" refers to the extra value that comes precisely from its being a whole, above and beyond the value of its parts. (Note he does not mention the value of a thing "down the whole," because Alice is hardly a thing, and it would hardly be polite to call her such, would it?)

This really doesn't add much Moore to what we knew before, but it does help us sort out some of the ideas. The members of the Rolling Stones each have their own value—especially Keith Richards, of course, but that hardly needed pointing out, did it now?—but put them all together and the band has a value "as a whole" that makes it more than the sum of its parts. Andrew Ridgely wasn't much on his own, but there was something magic—in terms of value "as a whole"—when he collaborated with George Michael that made Wham! more than just simply George plus Andrew (which is to say, George himself). Finally, the value of the Spice Girls "as a whole" must have been *very* high, given that the value of the individual members—judging from their solo "careers"—was, shall we say, *not* very high. (The "very" may be correct, but lo, the "high" is not!)

But the real benefit of this terminology is what it adds to the jam-yesterday-jam-tomorrow goods: if each momentary experience is bad, but the entire experience over time ("on the whole") is seen as good (either before or after), then the value of the collective experience "as a whole" must be tremendously high, right? After all, if you tot up all the negative bits, hour after hour or day after day, you arrive at quite a lot of negative value (or *disvalue*, as opposed to *datvalue*) that must be over-whelmed by quite a lot more positive value "as a whole" to end up with a positive value "on the whole."

But is that likely? (What—you don't know Lee? I rather like him, pleasant chap, though he doesn't fancy being com-pared to a butt.) It's a bit like asking if two wrongs make a right, isn't it? As a possible example, Moore suggests the institution of punishment, in which one evil—a crime, or an extended dance remix of the latest Andrew Ridgely single—is followed by another evil—punishment, or the ambient flip side of the aforementioned extended dance remix—presumably to serve justice (or to clear the dance floor for the 5:00 P.M. curling match).[13] But in that case, the second evil, punishment, may just as easily be considered a good, a duty of the state in fact, though outside of that particular context it would certainly be an evil. Recall that the White Queen asks Alice if she had ever been punished, to which Alice replied, "only for faults." The White Queen then says, "and you were all the better for it, I know!"[14] Fiddlesticks—we've gone and spoiled our example, but that simply confirms our judgment that two wrongs do *not* make a right.

Of course, that doesn't help us sort out the paradox of the jam-yesterday-jam-tomorrow goods—much less the con-tinued popularity of U2—but we cannot expect to solve the great puzzles of civilization today. (We've already done so much today, after all, and it's not even breakfast yet.) But let's move on to why Elijah Millgram brought up this puzzle in the first place (never one to settle for second place, to be sure)—procrastination.

I'll Write This Part Later . . .

To philosophers, procrastination is a puzzle of Carrollian mag-nitude, even though it is a strikingly common puzzle (kind of like Sudoku, but not as much fun)—after all, there must have been *some* reason why the White Rabbit was so late at the beginning of Alice's adventures! Another contemporary philosopher—and, in a wicked conspiracy, yet another Utahan hiking enthusiast—Chrisoula Andreou, defines procrastination as "those cases of delaying in which one leaves too late or puts off indefinitely what one should—relative to one's ends and information—have done sooner."[15] In other words, you know you should do something now, but nonetheless you put it off until later. That doesn't sound so odd, does it? We act against our better judgment all the time: we eat too many pastries, we indulge in too much drink, we sleep with too many . . . College students (raise your hands so we can see you, there you are) tend to be particularly frequent procrastinators, and presumably find the behavior even less puzzling. (Okay, you can put your hands down now.)

But philosophers are of a different sort, you see (and not just the hikers). As they see it, if a person judges a particular course of action to be best, and it is possible to take that course of action, then *of course* that person would take it; to do otherwise would be *irrational.*[16] But of even more course— or courser, if you would force her—that person, and many like her, do *not* take that course of action, choosing instead to eat that extra donut, watch that extra hour of *Survivor*—or put off doing whatever they need to do *now*. In general, this type of behavior is known as weakness of will or *akrasia*, and when it deals specifically with delaying activities, it becomes procrastination.[17]

So on the one hand we have behavior that is extremely common (even among the decidedly uncommon), but on the other hand is decidedly against commonsense thinking about how we make choices. It is into this rabbit-hole that Millgram eagerly leaps, arguing that much procrastination happens with respect to jam-yesterday-jam-tomorrow goods "because human motivation is relatively tightly tied to goods that are concretely visible in the moment (or moments). Not necessarily *this* moment: we are often (not always!) pretty good at deferring satisfaction when we can see a clear path to the later satisfaction, and when we can see that satisfaction, clothed in its apparent goodness or value, present at that later time. When the later or overall good, however, can only be seen (as it were) at the edges of one's peripheral vision—in the ways that jam-yesterday-jam-tomorrow goods typically are seen—motivation turns out to be relatively loosely tied to it."[18] So it's precisely because there is no jam today—and we *really* want jam today—that we procrastinate when it comes to doing things that only bring jam in the fuzzy, distant future.

For instance, I know that I'll look back fondly on the experience of teaching in the future, but somehow I can't summon those warm and fuzzy feelings when a stack of ungraded exams is staring me in the face (and *Spiceworld* is on TV again). Or, to use another anecdote of Millgram's, "someone may love her children, and love raising them, without feeling like getting out of bed to prepare breakfast, dress them, and get them off to school—even though raising children *is* mostly chores like that one." And this leads to procrastination: "If the good of the job, or of childraising, were visible in the moment, one would not have nearly the problems that so many people do in getting oneself to do the task of the moment. But the good is not visible in the moment . . . [so] a certain kind of procrastination is a perfectly understandable response to the structure of many important human goods."[19]

So What Do We Do, Then?

Okay, we understand why we procrastinate and end up wasting Time—*him*, of course, not it—but now what do we *do* about it? Is there any way to use the idea that many everyday goods have the jam-yesterday-jam-tomorrow nature to figure out how to get around that? Millgram has some answers for that too, couched in two examples: college graduations and (*sigh*) hiking.[20]

College graduations are odd things—rather like proces- sions, except no one lies down on his face, I should think—since often a student can "walk" in the ceremony even if she has not in fact finished her program requirements; if she doesn't finish them, then she walked for nothing (except maybe a little exer- cise and sun). And a student certainly doesn't have to attend graduation ceremonies to be awarded her degree—so what's it all about, then? Millgram offers up the answer that it provides motivation—a sometimes distant but clear one—for persisting in working toward your college education, which is, for most students, a jam-yesterday-jam-tomorrow good. (Many gradu- ates look back fondly at their college years, though I imagine the only experiences they enjoyed at the time were of a decidedly extracurricular nature, although often in the *spirit* of biology or chemistry.) As he very correctly notes, "If students had to make their own moment-to-moment decisions as to whether to read the book, or write the paper, or stay in the lecture, on the basis of its intangible contribution to their education, they would be all too likely to put off the unpleasant tasks to some other time."[21] So an elaborate ceremony is devised to provide a bright, shining light at the end of the tunnel, always there, to help motivate the unmotivated toward achieving it: not jam today, per se, but the "clear path to later satisfaction," which is almost as tasty (and certainly less filling).

With regard to hiking, the idea is even more direct: because hiking is a jam-yesterday-jam-tomorrow good, aspiring hikers are very likely to throw up their hands and say "Aw, let's turn around— my feet hurt, I'm sweaty, I'm not really from Utah anyway," and so on. But it turns out that popular trails—you know, the ones that picked on the smart trails in high school—have marked destinations, such as picturesque lookout points and rock for- mations, that provide a goal for the hiker, even though none of these is the "real" goal of hiking. ("Oh, honey, I'm so glad we saw those rocks that look like Bono *again*."[22]) "Nonetheless," writes Millgram, "these hikes go better when there is a designated goal that can serve as the turnaround point. It is easier to maintain the motivation required for a satisfying full day's hike . . . when there is a temporally localized end."[23] After all, even Alice told the Cheshire Cat that she didn't care where she went, as long as she went *"somewhere"*![24]

The point of these examples is that to prevent procrastination with respect to jam-yesterday-jam-tomorrow goods, you have to provide some sort of "jam today," a temporary, short-term goal, to motivate timely action. Rock formations and graduation ceremonies provide the "jam today" that motivates the hiker and the student to keep on plugging away, rather than putting off the hike or the studies to another day. Mind you, this is not a cure-all for every type of procrastination, but when it comes to jam-yesterday-jam-tomorrow goods, jam today seems like the obvious solution.

"Some People Have No More Sense Than a Baby!"[25]

In the end—no, don't close the book, we're not done yet—Alice didn't take the White Queen's generous offer of employment. But if she had, do you think she would have been in danger of procrastinating? Possibly not, because while there was "never jam today," there was a regular salary, which might have been enough to motivate young Alice to perform her duties with honor and timeliness. But in the real world—though there are days when I have my doubts about this whole "real world" thing, to tell you the truth (and don't get me started on "truth")—we do encounter a lot of jam-yesterday-jam-tomorrow goods. If Elijah Millgram has taught us anything—other than that all the *cool* philosophers hike—it is that we have a chance to beat this pattern if we recognize it for what it is, and make sure we have some sort of jam today to motivate us. But be careful of any jam that says "Eat Me"—go ask Alice![26]

NOTES

1. Lewis Carroll, *Through the Looking-Glass and What Alice Found There*, in *Alice's Adventures in Wonderland and Through the Looking-Glass* (Oxford: Oxford University Press, 1971), 174–175. All future citations from this collection will refer to one book or the other—never both and never neither, I assure you that.

2. Elijah Millgram, "Virtue for Procrastinators," in *The Thief of Time: Philosophical Essays on Procrastination*, Chrisoula Andreou and Mark D. White, eds. (Oxford: Oxford University Press, 2010), 151–164.

3. Oddly enough, Mr. Moore, named George Edward by his blessed parents, preferred to be called Bill, while the series editor of these fine volumes, Bill Irwin, prefers to be called Sally. To each his own I always say, except when I don't, in which case I still won't call him Sally.

4. G. E. Moore, *Principia Ethica* (Cambridge, UK: Cambridge University Press, 1903), 10.

5. Ibid., 27–31.

6. Ibid., 28. This entire quote is italicized in the original—he must have *really* meant it.

7. Moore faces quite a conundrum, however, in that the word "organic" had rather a different meaning at the time, thanks to "philosophers, especially those who profess to have derived great benefit from the writing of Hegel" (referring to the philosopher G. W. F. Hegel, 1770–1831, from whom I often profess to have derived great benefit, but at even greater cost). I think he—Moore, not Hegel—sounds rather Carrollesque when recounting his struggle with terminology: "I have said that the peculiar relation between part and whole which I have just been trying to define is one which has received no separate name. It would, however, be useful that it should have one; and there is a name, which might well be appropriated to it, if only it could be divorced from its present unfortunate usage" (ibid., 30).

8. Of course, everyone knows that the Spice Girls' 1996 hit "2 Becomes 1" was really a clever tribute to Moore and organic unities. (Honest—ones of the Mels told me once, though I can't seem to remember which.)

9. Moore, *Principia Ethica*, 28.

10. Ibid.

11. Yes, yes, I know, this is a book about *Alice in Wonderland*—but you've got to admit, the Spice Girls were almost absurd enough to have been in Lewis Carroll's classic children's books, right? (Say, Mr. Burton . . . have you met Miss Bunton?)

12. Moore, *Principia Ethica*, 214. Humpty Dumpty sounds quite the philosopher when he says, "when I use a word, it means just what I choose

it to mean—neither more nor less" (Carroll, *Through the Looking-Glass*, 190).

13. Moore, *Principia Ethica*, 216.
14. Carroll, *Through the Looking-Glass*, 176.
15. Chrisoula Andreou, "Understanding Procrastination," *Journal for the Theory of Social Behavior* 37 (2007), 183.
16. See Donald Davidson, "How Is Weakness of the Will Possible?" in his *Essays on Actions and Events* (Oxford: Oxford University Press, 1980), 21–42.
17. On weakness of will, see Sarah Stroud and Christine Tappolet, eds., *Weakness of Will and Practical Irrationality* (Oxford: Oxford University Press, 2003). Incidentally, Stroud has a chapter in *The Thief of Time* (51–67) titled "Is Procrastination Weakness of Will?" that argues that procrastination is not really weakness of will, but I can't seem to find it right now. . . . Ah, I'll find it later, though I know I should do it now, and I could do it now—if only my will were not so very weak. (Cheeky. . . .)
18. Millgram, "Virtue for Procrastinators," 155.
19. Ibid.
20. I think I'm ready to write for *Hiking and Philosophy*, don't you? But am I ready to move to Utah? I understand they *do* have jazz there.
21. Millgram, "Virtue for Procrastinators," 159.
22. Hmm . . . I guess it *is* possible to use the words "Bono" and "rocks" in the same sentence.
23. Millgram, "Virtue for Procrastinators," 159.
24. Carroll, *Alice's Adventures*, 57.
25. Thus saith Humpty Dumpty. See Carroll, *Through the Looking-Glass*, 185.
26. Now *that's* what I call a Slick ending.

NUCLEAR STRATEGISTS IN WONDERLAND

Ron Hirschbein

> Alice laughed. "There's no use trying," she said: "one
> *can't* believe impossible things."
>
> "I daresay you haven't had much practice," said the
> Queen. "When I was your age, I always did it for half-
> an-hour a day. Why, sometimes I've believed as many
> as six impossible things before breakfast."[1]

Join me as I chase strategists down the rabbit-hole and through
the looking glass into a realm bereft of empirical, logical, and
moral restraint. Attend the MAD (mutually assured destruction) tea party and play language games—you're it! Traffic in
euphemisms and buzzwords; get pelted with semantic quibbles
and peculiar riddles. Witness strange games, and try to believe
impossible things. Watch out for the Red Queen! Like the
strategists, she has a "thing" about decapitating enemies. But
don't panic when they play enemy cards—they're nothing but
a pack of cards, right? Finally, as you pass through the looking glass, you'll discover that you're real pawns on a fictional
chessboard—no rules.

We'll drop in on the strategists during that bipolar disorder known as the Cold War. We'll see what they were up to when the Cold War was getting hot, and we'll take a look at the cards they have up their sleeves during these latter days. But not so fast: You've got to mind your manners.

Nuclear Etiquette

> "I don't quite understand you," she said, as politely as she could.[2]

Don't embarrass yourself by trying to communicate in plain English. The psychologist Carol Cohn ventured down the rabbit-hole and spent a year in a strategic think tank. She learned Nukespeak but remembered her native tongue: "I vowed to speak English. . . . No matter how well informed my questions were . . . if I was speaking English rather than expert jargon, the men responded to me as though I were ignorant or simpleminded."[3]

Plain English is not spoken at either tea party. Alice could have been talking about strategic superstars when she declared: "The Hatter's remark seemed to have no sort of meaning in it, and yet it was certainly English." It wasn't Alice's fault, and it's not yours. Strategists play what Ludwig Wittgenstein (1889–1951) called bewitching language games. (*Alice in Wonderland* was in fact the Austrian philosopher's favorite piece of English prose.[4]) He wasn't thinking of Scrabble, and there's nothing pejorative about the language games we inevitably play. To proffer a philosophic distinction, there are games and then there are games. Let's judge the games in terms of their consequences. Certain games lead to nonsense or worse. That's why Wittgenstein vowed to teach you "to pass from a piece of disguised nonsense to something that is patent nonsense"[5] by refereeing language games.

Every language has a subset of specialized languages with unique rules and moves. Imagine: You eavesdrop on an exchange between two men talking about "A" and "D." Sure, they're communicating in English, but you're clueless until you realize this is linguistic shorthand—a language game—between a carpenter and his assistant: "A" means hammer, and "D" means nail—no problem. Such a game has good results—a new house. Now consider the philosophers Wittgenstein criticizes. (After attending a philosophy meeting, my son coined a term for such a group; said he: "You've heard of a parliament of owls; how 'bout a confusion of philosophers?") Wittgenstein was exercised by the games these confusions play—games ungrounded in verifiable facts. In disputes about ethereal notions such as free will, God, and immortality, according to Wittgenstein, these tradition-bound philosophers literally don't know what they're talking about. Nevertheless, there are peculiar rules and career moves essential to play a never-ending game, a contest that can be neither lost nor won. Enchanted by the language itself, such games lead to interminable confusion, if not nonsense. Strategists, like these traditional philosophers, play private language games. Disconnected from reality, these games move on their own momentum—if only the results were mere confusion.

So don't worry about the facts. There are none. As the philosopher Jacques Derrida (1930–2004) says with uncharacteristic clarity: "A nuclear war has not taken place: one can only talk and write about it."[6] There are no facts about nuclear war-fighting, and (as we shall see) the "fact" that nuclear arsenals *necessarily* prevent war is based upon a common fallacy. As Bernard Brodie (an early strategist) reminded his colleagues, no one has experienced a nuclear exchange: "In the contest of thermonuclear war, everything is new and every military arm or weapon is essentially untested."[7]

Wittgenstein wisely warned: "What we cannot speak about we must pass over in silence."[8] Strategists aren't silent. They call their make-believe stories "scenarios"—it gives them gravitas. Lewis Carroll wrote a similar genre of literary nonsense—but he realized what he was doing.

We must make haste if we're to catch the rabbit. There's no time to master Nuclear Jabberwocky. The party is about to start. I can only offer a few more tips. Alice was an ingénue prone to faux pas. You can avoid such indiscretions by candy-coating your conversation with sophisticated euphemisms. Remember, strategists are wannabe realists allergic to reality:

- The United States didn't drop atomic bombs on Japan; it used two *devices*—Fat Man and Little Boy—to end the war. (These names sound like hamburger combos at Big Boy, not weapons of mass destruction.)
- Never say "War Department"; the name was changed to Department of Defense with the advent of the Atomic Age. In fact, don't talk of war at all—sounds like someone could get hurt.
- It's gauche to mention civilian deaths. It's just collateral damage (no worse than a sub-600 credit score).
- Remember, the name of the MX missile was changed to "Peacekeeper." (It's fitted with ten 500,000 kt "peaceheads.")
- Our devices are defensive, a nuclear umbrella—comfort in an inclement international clime. Theirs are offensive.
- Never forget, any strategy—no matter how provocative—is always a deterrent. Deterrence does not merely defend the homeland against aggression; it *prevents* aggression through unfriendly persuasion.

The Mad Tea Party

"But I don't want to go among mad people," Alice remarked.

"Oh, you can't help that," said the Cat: "we're all mad here. I'm mad. You're mad."

"How do you know I'm mad?" said Alice.

"You must be," said the Cat, "or you wouldn't have come here."[9]

Like Alice, you'll have to crash the party—especially if you need a haircut. Only like-minded men are invited. The party, of course, begins with a riddle: *Why is it safe to have weapons of a kind and number it is not safe to use?*[10] Strategists answer with Churchill's encomium to apocalyptic weapons. In the world according to Churchill, the prospect of mutually assured destruction ushers in a miracle surpassing the promise of Christianity—peace on Earth *without* goodwill toward men. "By a process of sublime irony [we] have reached a state where safety will be the sturdy child or terror, and survival the twin brother of annihilation."[11]

Philosophers are a little touchy about language and logic: eloquence is no substitute for dubious reasoning. In plain English, Churchill and the others are saying: *To reduce the risk of nuclear war, the risk must be increased.* The philosopher Richard Rorty (1931–2007) would call this contradiction (or paradox, to be charitable) the strategists' final vocabulary. This notion of deterrence is the self-evident, final word at the MAD tea party. Unlike philosophers—vexed by radical and persistent self-doubt—strategists don't "question the platitudes which encapsulate the use of a given final vocabulary." The philosopher worries "about the possibility that she has been initiated into the wrong tribe [or] taught to play the wrong language game."[12]

Like Alice, philosophers are troubled by contradictions and unintelligible prose, especially when no effort is made to resolve the contradictions and to render clear and distinct expression. Lewis Carroll was amused by contradictions; Wittgenstein was bemused; but the strategist Edward Luttwak (an influential Pentagon advisor) is bewitched. Carroll's literary nonsense frees us from the constraints of logic and common sense for a few merry hours. Luttwak's nonsense mocks logical and empirical analysis of the obdurate realities of the nuclear age.

> Strategic practice can be freed from the misleading influence of common sense logic. . . . This offers the prospect of an eventual liberation from the false disciplines of consistency and coherence.[13]

This is not an invitation for an excursion into Hegelian dialectics (1770–1831) that resolves contradictions. Hegel, followed by Marx (1818–1883), argued that the contradictions inherent in thought and life are dynamic, and can generate a grand synthesis that resolves the contradiction. (Marx hoped that worsening contradictions of capitalism would be resolved by socialism—we're still hoping.)

But like the Mad Hatter, Luttwak finds amazing grace in *irresolvable* contradictions. He reiterates a Latin proverb: "If you would have peace, prepare for war."[14] But why not: *If you would have war, prepare for war?* Such a discussion might end the bewitchment of Luttwak's language game.

Strategists prepare for war. They play dangerous games. A balancing act—Delicate Balance of Terror—is a favorite language game.[15] Strategists depart from reality and go on a magical mystery tour where abstractions only refer to other abstractions. (When "terrorism" got bad press the name was changed to "balance of power" to protect the guilty.) What's the proper balance of terror? Wittgenstein warned against trying to resolve such irresolvable confusion. Just how much terror is essential to assure that "safety will be the sturdy child of terror?" The question is hotly disputed. Too little and the Soviets won't get the message—be afraid, be terribly afraid; too much and the Soviets have incentive to strike first. (If this dispute reminds you about conjectures about how many angels can dance on the head of a pin, you got it right.) Balance makes sense when you think of laboratory scales or algebraic equations— check the weights or do the math. But how can disputes about balance between nuclear forces be resolved? Indeed, can terror— let alone sufficient nuclear terror—be properly defined, let alone reckoned?

Both Lewis Carroll and Ludwig Wittgenstein would recognize such disputes as bewitching language games played with meaningless words—literary nonsense. Such nonsense delights Carroll, angers Wittgenstein, and drives strategists to the brink of the abyss.

Did the Mad Hatter and the others pretend to be mad to bedevil Alice? Was this Carroll's playful intention? Who knows? We do know that on occasion American officials considered feigning madness to bedevil enemies—it gets curiouser and curiouser. Nixon took a turn at Let's Pretend to Be Mad. According to Nixon confidant H. R. Haldeman, the president toyed with playing the madman card to exact concessions from the Vietnamese.

> We were walking along a foggy beach. . . . He [Nixon] said, "I call it the Madman theory, Bob. I want the North Vietnamese to believe I've reached the point where I might do anything to stop the war. We'll just slip the word to them that, for god's sake, you know Nixon is obsessed with Communism. We can't restrain him when he's angry—and he has his hand on the nuclear button."[16]

Strategists aren't really mad, but they get recklessly high when they reach for that bottle marked DRINK THIS! Is a 12-step program necessary to cure their addiction? Fred Iklé, a strategist and policymaker, thinks so:

> Strategic analysis works like a narcotic. It dulls our senses of moral outrage about the tragic confrontation of nuclear arsenals primed . . . to unleash widespread genocide.[17]

Iklé has reason to worry. Strategists such as Thomas Schelling play a game *they* call Russian roulette.[18] (Someone needs to make a video entitled "Strategists Gone Wild.") Schelling boasts that he and his Pentagon colleagues risked nuclear war by confronting the Soviets in Berlin and Cuba. Here's how they think. Here's how the world could end with a bang, not a whimper—Lewis Carroll would love it: "He thinks we think he'll attack, so he thinks we shall, so he will, so we must."[19] During the Cold War every president took his chances and spun the barrel.[20]

By all accounts the world came closest to a nuclear confla-
gration during the Cuban missile crisis. Khrushchev unexpectedly backed down—better red than dead. Schelling stared into
the abyss and liked what he saw. He's sure that jousting on the
brink taught the Soviets a lesson: a resolute America could win
the competition in Russian roulette.[21]

More fearful strategists allow that things could go wrong;
deterrence could fail. Accordingly, they conjure up civil
defense plans. Now, neither Alice's Wonderland nor Nuclear
Wonderland are drug-free environments. Unable to say
"No!," Alice experimented. Once upon a time strategists
stashed 60 million doses of morphine to ease unfortunate
survivors into the next world. This program (which smacked
of realism) was flushed down the toilet when Nancy Reagan
began her War on Drugs.[22]

We don't know what the Caterpillar was smoking in his
confrontation with Alice. But you'll wonder what the authors
of a Lawrence Livermore National Laboratory study were
smoking if you read *Worker Protection for a Nuclear Attack with
30 Minutes (or Less) Warning*. (I doubt the White Queen would
believe it.) According to the study, you can survive a nuclear
attack—*even at ground zero*—if you jump in the lake: "Jump
into a deep body of water and swim (at least 3 or 4 feet under
the surface) for as long as possible while periodically coming
up for air."[23] The study recommends practicing your aquatic
skills and dressing appropriately in cold water. The authors
recognize that deep bodies of water may be unavailable. All is
not lost. Workers could pile on top of one another, increasing
the prospects of survival for those on the bottom. (Workers of the
world, unite! You have nothing to lose but your lives.)

Now there are sages at the party who allow that MAD
doesn't work in theory. Admittedly, it's beset by contradictions, imaginary abstractions, make-believe, and reckless
risk-taking—but no need to jump in the lake. Deterrence

through mutually assured destruction doesn't work in theory, but it works in practice. The argument is simple indeed:

1. America has had a nuclear arsenal since 1945.
2. No war occurred between America and the Soviet Union after 1945.
3. Therefore, the arsenal deterred World War III.

Gasp! The classic *Post hoc ergo propter hoc* fallacy (*After this, therefore because of this*). Beginning logic students get it: The rooster crowing doesn't make the sun come up. Some prominent officials recognize the fallacy. Admiral Eugene Carroll (a NATO commander) warned:

> It does not follow that war has been deterred solely by the nuclear threat. There are many, many other practical military, political and economic factors which weigh against superpower conflict far more effective than the incredible abstraction of nuclear deterrence.[24]

By and large, strategists ignore alternative explanations; worse yet, they overlook the obvious: correlation doesn't *necessarily* prove causation. You're unwelcome at the MAD tea party unless you're a true believer: *only* the American nuclear arsenal prevented World War III. Like Alice, to get along at the party, you must overlook the obvious. You can't, so you become a provocateur.

You urge that, according to the strategists' reasoning, the nuclear arsenal prevented war between America and Canada. To believe such nonsense you must overlook a salient fact: Except for some unpleasantry during the War of 1812, there's no precedent for warfare between these nations. So why overlook another salient fact? With the exception of the American invasion of Siberia in 1919, there's no precedent for warfare between America and the Soviet Union.

You're wound up; you're on a roll. You remind the strategists that in order to prove that nukes keep the peace, they'd need to build a time machine, return to 1945, remove nuclear weapons from the scene, and witness the results. (Even the Pentagon might not finance such a boondoggle.) It's no use. Strategic language games are immune to criticism. Echoing Alice, you vow: "I'll never go *there* again! . . . It is the stupidest tea-party I ever was at in all my life!"[25]

Now you're in serious trouble: meet the Queen of Hearts.

The Queen of Hearts as Nuclear Strategist

> The Queen had only one way of settling all difficulties, great or small. "Off with his head!" she said, without even looking around.[26]

Like the Queen of Hearts, strategists are obsessed. During the Cold War they advocated weapons designed to decapitate Soviet leadership. Ever since Barry Goldwater quipped about lobbing a bomb into the Kremlin's men's room, strategists fantasized about beheading the leaders of the Evil Empire. Dick Cheney and Donald Rumsfeld successfully promoted the strategy: "A core element of the Reagan Administration's strategy for fighting a nuclear war would be to decapitate the Soviet leadership by striking at top political and military officials."[27]

The unexpectedly peaceful demise of the Soviet Union left an enemy gap. Were nukes still needed? The strategists had more cards up their sleeves—they played enemy cards. The Iraq War revived an old custom: picturing enemies on playing cards. Like Alice, you'll encounter a pack of cards. During the bad old days of the Cold War, strategists played Joseph Stalin, Nikita Khrushchev, Mao Zedong, and Ho Chi Minh. These days they play Saddam Hussein, Osama bin Laden, and Mahmoud Ahmadinejad.

But look closely at the cards. What do you see? Like the Cheshire Cat, Hitler's visage appears time and again. The Austrian painter turned fuehrer is an immortal enemy reincarnated in America's enemies, real or imagined. Both Bush administrations warned that Hussein was Hitler reincarnated, and lately we hear that the new Hitler speaks Farsi.

Nuclear weapons were developed in response to Hitler's ascendancy, and the arsenal is updated in response to Hitler's ersatz immortality. He's the ideal enemy: powerful and murderous, a psychopath bereft of humanity—justly feared and hated. This most formidable enemy argues for the most formidable weapons.

The Queen of Hearts is still shouting. Ignore her. Don't swallow the propaganda that makes enemies appear larger than life—and death. When they play the Hitler card, remember Alice's grownup grasp of reality:

> "Off with her head!" the Queen shouted at the top of her voice. Nobody moved.
>
> "Who cares for you?" said Alice, (she had grown to her full size by this time.) "You're nothing but a pack of cards!"[28]

Grand Masters of the Universe

> Alice stood without speaking, looking out in all directions over the country—and a most curious country it was . . . It's marked out in all directions like a chessboard . . .
>
> "It's a great huge game of chess that's being played—all over the world."[29]

Join Alice on her final adventure through the looking glass. It will leave you speechless. Gaze upon the strategists' global game—there *is* a certain finality about it. The men who control the fate of the Earth have indeed marked out the planet in all directions—like a chessboard. It's a match played all over the world, but we're not the players. We live in a time of great decisions, but we're not making any.

Poor Alice: invisible to strange, indifferent forces operating against her will and behind her back. She craved recognition, *any* recognition, even that of a feckless pawn. Her fictional wish is our unnerving reality: We *are* pawns—expendable pawns. Herman Kahn (whose avatar is Dr. Strangelove) makes the point in a work praised by Brent Scowcroft and the redoubtable Donald Rumsfeld:

> The possibility—both menacing and perversely comforting—that even if 300 million people were killed in a nuclear war, there would still be more than 4 billion left alive. . . . And a power that attains significant strategic superiority is likely to survive the war, perhaps even "win" . . . by extending its hegemony—at least for a time—over much of the world.[30]

You'll witness a bizarre version of speed chess: a contest with uncanny resemblance to the arms race. The pieces are governed by their own rules, and strange new pieces are played as the arms race accelerates and deploys new weapons. Mirroring Alice's Wonderland, the arms race moves faster and faster, but everything stays the same—America's unprecedented vulnerability to nuclear destruction. No clever strategy, no knockoff of Star Wars fantasy weapons, resolves the nuclear predicament—*America lies defenseless.* The players should have learned that the only way to win is not to play the game.

Like Alice, the nuclear strategists went down into an unknown world "never once considering how in the world . . . [they] would get out again."[31] Alice's adventures came to an end, a happy ending at that—she escaped the madness and returned to innocent childhood. But alas, no happy ending is assured for us expendable pawns caught in the strategic game.

We're real characters entrapped in the strategists' fiction—a never-ending story.

NOTES

1. Lewis Carroll, *Through the Looking-Glass and What Alice Found There* (Philadelphia: Henry Altemus Company, 1887), 102–103.
2. Lewis Carroll, *Alice's Adventures in Wonderland* (London: Macmillan, 1898), 100.
3. Carol Cohn, "Nuclear Language and How We Learned to Pat the Bomb,"*Bulletin of the Atomic Scientists* (June 1987): 22. I'm indebted to Cohn's account of her year spent at a strategic think tank.
4. See Ludwig Wittgenstein, *Philosophical Investigations* (New York: Macmillan, 1965) for a full account of language games. A number of authors draw connections between *Alice* and Wittgenstein. See, for example, Christopher Barry Gray, "Alice in Wittgenstein,"*Journal of Value Inquiry* 29 (1985): 77–88.
5. Ludwig Wittgenstein, *Philosophical Investigations: The German Text with a Revised English Translation*, 3rd edition, trans. G. E. M. Anscombe (Malden, MA: Wiley-Blackwell, 2001), 113.
6. Quoted by John Canaday in *The Nuclear Muse* (Madison: University of Wisconsin Press, 2000), 222.
7. Bernard Brodie, "Influence of Mass Destruction Weapons on Strategy," delivered at the Naval War College, May 3, 1956. [Reprinted in the National Security Archive's Nuclear History Project.]
8. Ludwig Wittgenstein, *Tractatus Logico-Philosophicus*, trans. D. F. Pears and B. F. McGuinness (London and New York: Routledge, 2001), 89.
9. Carroll, *Alice's Adventures*, 90.
10. This riddle emerges from an insight in Cohn.
11. Quoted in "Minimum Nuclear Deterrence," SAIC Strategic Group, Washington, D.C., May 15, 2003.
12. Richard Rorty, "Ironists and Metaphysicians," in *The Truth about the Truth*, ed. Walter Truett Anderson (New York: Putnam, 1995), 101–102.
13. Edward Luttwak, *Strategy: The Logic of War and Peace* (Cambridge: Harvard University Press, 1987), 3.
14. Ibid.
15. See Albert Wohlstetter's influential "The Delicate Balance of Terror," in *Foreign Affairs* 37 (January 1959): 211–234.
16. See Louis Beres's account of this episode in *Apocalypse* (Chicago: University of Chicago Press, 1980), 68–70.

17. Quoted by Greg Herken in *Counsels of War* (New York: Oxford University Press, 1987), 349.

18. Quoted by Richard K. Betts in *Nuclear Blackmail and Nuclear Balance* (Washington, D.C.: The Brookings Institution, 1987), 1.

19. Thomas C. Schelling, *The Strategy of Conflict* (New York: Oxford University Press, 1963), 207–209.

20. Betts, *Nuclear Blackmail and Nuclear Balance* (Washington: The Brookings Institution, 1987).

21. See my account of this episode in "The Essence of Indecision" in my *What If They Gave a Crisis and Nobody Came?* (Westwood: Praeger, 1997).

22. *New York Times*, July 3, 2009, 3.

23. David W. Gregg, *Worker Protection for a Nuclear Attack with 30 Minutes (or Less)Warning* (Washington: National Technical Information Service, 1984), 6.

24. Eugene Carroll, "Nuclear Weapons and Deterrence," in *The Nuclear Crisis Reader*, ed. Gwyn Prins (New York: Vintage, 1984), 4.

25. Carroll, *Alice's Adventures*, 74.

26. Ibid., 125.

27. James Mann, "The Armageddon Plan,"*The Atlantic Monthly* (March 2004), 31.

28. Carroll, *Alice's Adventures*, 116.

29. Carroll, *Through the Looking-Glass*, 46.

30. Herman Kahn, *Thinking about the Unthinkable in the 1980s* (New York: Simon and Schuster, 1984), 93.

31. Carroll, *Through the Looking-Glass*, 46.

"YOU'RE NOTHING BUT A PACK OF CARDS!": ALICE DOESN'T HAVE A SOCIAL CONTRACT

Dennis Knepp

Alice finally escapes Wonderland when, after growing "more than a mile high" (in the words of the King of Hearts), she attacks the members of this most absurd court.[1] Normally it's wrong to attack the members of a court of law, but Alice's circumstances are anything but normal. Alice is completely correct to attack these cards who wish to do her harm.

It's not just the crazy cast of characters. It's not just the unfair verdict. There's more to it. The basic idea of rule of law does not apply to Alice. She is not part of their world. She does not have a social contract in Wonderland.

A "social contract" is a theory of political philosophy that answers the question "Why should I obey the law?" or "Why do we even have laws?" A social contract is an implicit agreement to obey the law. It is implicit because we don't say out loud, "I promise to obey the law." It's unsaid. We just assume it.

In a free society like ours, you basically have three choices. You can leave. You can try to change the laws. Or you can do neither and implicitly agree to obey the laws. That's a social contract.

This idea goes all the way back to the trial of Socrates (469–399 BCE) in ancient Athens.[2] Despite thinking that the jury was against him before the trial began, Socrates accepted the guilty verdict—on the charge of corrupting the youth— and its terrible penalty: death. But why so? Because he agreed to live by their rules even without explicitly saying so. He was born there, raised there, educated there, and protected there. He even fought in the army defending Athens. He never left and he never tried to change the laws. In short, Socrates made a social contract with Athens—an implicit agreement to follow their laws no matter what the outcome.

But this doesn't apply to Alice. She wasn't born in Wonderland; she wasn't raised there or educated there. And she's not an immigrant who moves in willingly—she literally fell into the place! Of the three options in a free society (leave, change things, or implicitly agree to obey), Alice is desperately trying to leave. She does not have an implicit agreement to obey, so she doesn't have a social contract. She has every right to use violence against the court.

Lewis Carroll would have known about the trial and death of Socrates. He was a classically educated Englishman.

The Young Dodgson's Classical Education

"Lewis Carroll" is the pen name of Charles Lutwidge Dodgson (1832–1898). After Charles Dodgson (Lewis Carroll) died, his brothers and sisters approached Stuart Dodgson Collingwood, a relative who knew Charles, and asked him to write a biography.[3]

As the biography reveals, the young Charles's education included the Latin classics. When he was twelve years old,

Charles was sent to Richmond School.[4] Collingwood writes in his biography: "As was the custom at that time, Charles began to compose Latin verses at a very early age, his first copy being dated November 25, 1844."[5] Collingwood then quotes six lines of Charles's Latin verse "on the subject of evening" and then scoffs at the grammatical mistakes. These men lived in a time and place where reading Latin poetry was normal. We don't. And since Collingwood doesn't tell me what the mistakes are, I can only marvel that a twelve-year-old boy could even try to write six lines of Latin verse.

In February 1846, Charles was sent to Rugby School.[6] While there he created several different magazines for school-wide circulation. When he was seventeen or eighteen years old he created *The Rectory Umbrella*. Collingwood writes: "The best thing in *The Rectory Umbrella* was a parody on Lord Macaulay's style in the 'Lays of Ancient Rome'; Charles had a special aptitude for parody, as is evidenced by several of the best-known verses in his later books."[7]

So, as a teenager Charles was already writing parodies of his classical education. As Lewis Carroll, he would end Alice's adventures with an absurd trial. Even without Carroll saying it, his readers would think of the trial of Socrates because they all shared a classical education.

A Paradoxical Martyr for Free Speech

The weird and defiant Socrates has been a hero for philosophers and dissidents throughout history. Socrates himself wrote nothing. He talked instead. He frequently hung out at the Athenian *agora*. That Greek word is usually translated as "marketplace," but that might make it sound like he spent his days at the grocery store. It's better to think of Socrates in the town square.

Many older small towns in America (ones that grew prior to World War II) still have a town square. That's where everything important happens. That's where they have public parties (like Fourth of July fireworks). It's where to get the best gossip. It's where you find the farmer's market on Saturday mornings. It's where car shows take place. It's where a parade would start. It's the place to be to be connected to life in your town.

And the ancient Athenians prized being connected. They invented participatory democracy open to all citizens (not just the rich!), and those who did not participate were called *idios* or "private." In this vibrant and hopping place, the eccentric Socrates talked and argued with everyone. He saw himself on a divine mission to get the prosperous Athenians to question their beliefs about virtue and the nature of the soul.

But while Socrates was a product of this open and stimulating democracy, he was also a sharp critic of it. Socrates admired the closed and intolerant rival city, Sparta. When he questioned people about goodness or courage or justice, it always turned out that their responses were conflicting or vague. Socrates was always able to find some example or situation that made their beliefs look inadequate. That's really no surprise. Even today, most people try to be a good person even if they can't define what it means to be a good person in every conceivable circumstance.

Here's a variation on a favorite example in ethics. Ethics is the part of philosophy that deals with studying goodness and related value terms. We usually say "Honesty is the best policy," and my wife and I teach our children to always tell the truth. It seems obvious that a good person should tell the truth. Now suppose that the Queen of Hearts took my Logic course and failed. This would come as no surprise, since Carroll's characters are delightfully illogical. Anyway, suppose that an angry Queen of Hearts (with a company of armed card soldiers) rings my doorbell. My wife, Jen, answers. The Queen asks to see me regarding her failing grade in Logic. Jen can see the company of armed card soldiers and she knows of the Queen's habit of beheading anyone who displeases her. What should Jen do?

She knows that a good person should tell the truth, but she also knows that a lie would protect me. How is it that being a good person results in the wrong answer? How is it possible that doing the right thing sometimes means not being a good person? What does it mean to be a good person?

I don't know the answers. Ethics is difficult business. And in ancient Athens, their attempts to define fundamental philosophical ideas always failed under the negative dialectical scrutiny of Socrates. I. F. Stone (1907–1989) writes: "For Socrates, if you couldn't define something with unvarying comprehensiveness, then you really didn't know what it was."[8] And if the Athenians didn't know what it meant to be good or courageous or just, then they shouldn't have been running the city. Socrates was against democracy, favoring instead a benign dictatorship under one who knows the correct definitions of goodness and courage and justice.

Although Socrates himself just talked and talked, some of his admirers took action and helped in temporary overthrows of the democracy. For this and much more, Socrates at the age of seventy was brought up on charges of impiety and corrupting youth, found guilty, and sentenced to death by poisoning. He was an early victim of the democratic irony that in a free society one should be free to openly criticize the free society. Socrates paradoxically manages to be both a martyr for free speech and an opponent of free speech.[9]

One might think that Socrates would openly condemn the court and its laws. But he doesn't. He accepts the verdict. He embraces his impending doom. Later his friend Crito tries to bust Socrates out of prison. In Plato's *Crito* the old philosopher convinces us that he should stay. Socrates explains to Crito that since he never tried to leave, and he never tried to change the laws, he must stay and obey no matter the outcome. He has a social contract with Athens. Because he has an obligation to obey the laws, he will not break out of prison. He will abide by the verdict of the court.

Why the Queen of Hearts Must Yell

Other classically educated Englishmen, like the philosopher Thomas Hobbes (1588–1679), read about the trial and death of Socrates. Hobbes, in fact, wrote a revival of Socrates' social contract theory in his 1651 masterpiece *Leviathan*.[10] Hobbes was a generation younger than Shakespeare (1564–1616) and saw the *King James Bible* published in 1611. Hobbes writes philosophy with that great King Jamesian English, and I love to read his books.

Hobbes's first book was a translation of Thucydides'*History of the Peloponnesian War.* Thucydides is our eyewitness to the brutal fight between the Athenians and the Spartans during that golden age of fifth-century BCE Greece. That's the time of Socrates. Like Carroll, Hobbes was an Englishman educated in the classics.

In *Leviathan* Hobbes argues that there must be a ruthless supreme monarch who terrorizes the people into following the social contract. Basically, without the fear of getting caught, people would break the rules all the time. So fear of punishment for breaking the laws makes people follow the law and keep the social contract. If you break the social contract, then you are outside the security of law and in Nature's violent world. The supreme monarch can use any form of destruction against lawbreakers, since they have moved themselves outside the safety of society's laws.

That's the Queen of Hearts. What's her first scene? The Two, Five, and Seven of Spades are found painting the roses on the trees.[11] They are trying to deceive her. No one deceives the Queen! It is subversion. The rebels must be dealt with quickly and publicly. "Off With Their Heads!" The offenders are like a cancer that must be cut out. More important, the other cards must be terrorized. They must see the consequences of upsetting the queen so that they will never *never* **never** want to upset the Queen. Law and order must be established with a display of violence. As Hobbes writes: "And Covenants, without the Sword, are but Words, and of no strength to secure a man at all."[12]

Don't feel sorry for those terrorized cards. Thomas Hobbes and the Queen of Hearts would argue that it is for their own good. They need to belong to a pack. I mean, really, a Two, Five, or Seven of Spades is worthless all alone. If you're playin' poker, they would be valuable as part of a flush or something. But that's only with more cards. Cards get value together with other cards—with being part of a full deck. A single, solitary card is totally worthless.

Hobbes writes that solitary life outside the security of the social contract is worse than horrible. You can't trust anyone. Nature is constant warfare.

> In such condition, there is no place for Industry; because the fruit thereof is uncertain; and consequently no Culture of the Earth; no Navigation, nor use of the commodities that may be imported by Sea; no commodious Building; no Instruments of moving, and removing such things as require much force; no Knowledge of the face of the Earth; no account of Time; no Arts; no Letters; no Society; and which is worst of all, continuall feare, and dangers of violent death; And the life of man, solitary, poore, nasty, brutish, and short.[13]

Hobbes argues that people must give up their natural liberty to survive together in a society, and that we need a ruthlessly violent absolute monarch who will terrorize everyone into obeying society's social contract. The cards need the Queen of Hearts. She *should* scream her orders of execution so that everyone hears and is terrorized into submission. A quiet and private execution won't do. Her screams terrorize the cards and keep the deck full. Outside the safety of the social contract is the violence of Nature. She must yell *"Off with their heads!"* It's for their own good. It keeps them safe.

Some real leaders think that violent oppression is necessary for society. Kim Jong-il presents himself as protecting the North Koreans as thousands of them starve in hard labor camps. Adolf Hitler described himself as protecting the Aryan race with a war that killed millions of them. Both Mao Zedong and Joseph Stalin killed millions of their citizens while creating communist utopias for them. Lots of ruthless tyrants terrorize the people, supposedly for their own good. The Queen of Hearts works as satire because there are real examples to satirize!

Is There a Better Approach?
The Queen Scares Me!

Yes. There is. We could democratically elect our leaders by voting, limit their power by diffusing authority into three branches of government (executive, legislative, and judicial), and then throw the bums out if they become maniacal megalomaniacs.

That's the basic idea of the *Two Treatises of Government* (1689), written by another classically educated Englishman: John Locke (1632–1704).[14] Locke accepts Hobbes's basic idea that we must band together to protect ourselves and that we need a central authority to enforce the social contract. But he adds that a legitimate government must be limited in power and rule with the consent of the governed. The individual person has value. An individual has *rights* that no government can take away. Whew! That makes all the difference.

John Locke's book greatly influenced Thomas Jefferson (1743–1826) and his writing of the Declaration of Independence (1776). Out with King George III and in with President George Washington! We have no kings here in the United States. No divinely appointed hereditary monarchs. No absolute dictators. No rule through terror. We have a president whose power is limited and whose tenure is short.

Both liberals and conservatives in the United States use Locke's social contract theory. The Harvard-based philosopher John Rawls (1921–2002) used a social contract theory in his 1971 *A Theory of Justice*.[15] Rawls has us imagine making the social contract without knowing who we will be in the society. He argues that if we didn't know whether we'd be rich or poor, we'd agree to maximize the well-being of the least well-off in society just in case that turns out to be us. Basically Rawls is justifying President Lyndon Johnson's Great Society War on Poverty.

By contrast, when Republicans took over the House of Representatives on November 8, 1994, they purposely called their plan a "Contract with America."[16] Their understanding of the social contract led them to conclude that President Lyndon Johnson's Great Society War on Poverty stifled individual initiative and penalized successful people with high taxes. As speaker of the House of Representatives, Newt Gingrich first used the legislative branch to impede President Clinton. Clinton's doublespeak caught up with him regarding his relationship with White House intern Monica Lewinsky, and so the Republicans used the court system.

The court! That's where we started. That's where we left Alice. Okay, so the court system is a check against the powerful—it is an essential part of Locke's political philosophy. It's needed. But I wrote that Alice is justified in attacking the court. Doesn't that destroy the court's ability to stop the powerful?

A Closer Look at Alice's Trial

The court of the King and Queen of Hearts isn't a check against the powerful. It's run by the powerful! So it's not like Locke's separation of powers at all. It's much more like Hobbes's reign of terror.

Alice is not on trial. The Knave of Hearts is. Alice is a witness. She's more like Crito—Socrates' friend who tried unsuccessfully to bust the old philosopher out of prison. Socrates introduces the social contract to explain why he must accept the verdict. But the Knave of Hearts does no such thing.

Instead, the Knave of Hearts rightfully protests. Further evidence is presented: a note sent to somebody (since it obviously can't be to nobody!). The White Rabbit says that it's not written in the Knave's handwriting. The King explains that the Knave imitated someone else. The Knave protests: "I didn't write it, and they can't prove that I did: there's no name signed at the end."[17] The King declares that this is the clinching proof since an honest man would have signed his note!

Alice gives the correct analysis: "It doesn't prove anything of the sort!"[18] After challenging the King on the content of the note, the White Rabbit reads their nonsense verses and the King provides an even more nonsensical interpretation. The jury is then told ("for about the twentieth time that day"[19]) to consider their verdict. But the Queen wants the sentence first. When Alice disagrees with having the sentence before the verdict, the Queen yells her final "Off with her head!"[20] That's when Alice rejects the whole court with "You're nothing but a pack of cards!"[21] When the cards attack, she rightfully defends herself.

This isn't Locke's court as a check against the powerful. The Queen is Hobbes's ruthless dictator, and the threat of beheading terrorizes the cards into submission.

In Hobbes's system, restrictions on violence only exist within the confines of the law. Outside that, anything goes. Alice isn't part of their world. As her own more-than-a-mile-high Leviathan, Alice stands outside their social contract. She's not part of a full deck. Outside the social contract is Nature, where there are no restrictions on violence. Alice is correct to defend herself any way she can. If she doesn't, her life will be "nasty, brutish, and short."

NOTES

1. *Alice's Adventures in Wonderland* was originally published in 1865. For this essay, I'll be using *The Annotated Alice: Alice's Adventures in Wonderland and Through the Looking-Glass*, by Lewis Carroll, with an introduction and notes by Martin Gardner (New York: Bramhall House, 1960). The King calls Alice "more than a mile high" in chapter XII, "Alice's Evidence," 156.
2. Plato (428 BCE–328 BCE) is the primary author for most of our knowledge about the trial and death of Socrates—especially his *Euthyphro*, *Apology*, *Crito*, and *Phaedo*. My take on Socrates' life and trial is heavily influenced by I. F. Stone's *The Trial of Socrates* (New York: Doubleday, 1989).
3. "It is with no undue confidence that I have accepted the invitation of the brothers and sisters of Lewis Carroll to write this Memoir" (Stuart Dodgson Collingwood, *The Life and Letters of Lewis Carroll* [New York: The Century Co., 1898], republished by Gale Research Company [Detroit: Book Tower, 1967], ix).
4. Collingwood, *Life and Letters*, 21.
5. Ibid., 23.
6. Ibid., 26.
7. Ibid., 36.
8. Stone, *The Trial of Socrates*, 68. That's the opening line of the appropriately titled chapter 6: "A Wild Goose Chase: The Socratic Search for Truth."
9. I. F. Stone argues that Socrates could have made a free speech argument, since after all he is just talking. But he didn't because he doesn't believe in free speech. See Stone, *The Trial of Socrates*, chapter. 15: "How Socrates Easily Might Have Won Acquittal."
10. Thomas Hobbes, *Leviathan*, 1651. A good version is edited by Richard Tuck for *Cambridge Texts in the History of Political Thought* (New York: The Press Syndicate of the University of Cambridge, 1996).
11. Carroll, *Annotated Alice*, 105–110. I hope you get the joke that the Spade cards are the gardeners.
12. Hobbes, *Leviathan*, 117.
13. Ibid., 89. It's Hobbes's 1651 spelling for 'continuall feare' and 'poore.'
14. John Locke, *Two Treatises of Government*, 1689. A good version is edited by Peter Laslett for *Cambridge Texts in the History of Political Thought* (Cambridge University Press, 1988).
15. John Rawls, *A Theory of Justice* (Cambridge, MA: Harvard University Press, 1971).

16. *Contract with America: The Bold Plan by Rep. Newt Gingrich, Rep. Dick Armey, and the House Republicans to Change the Nation*, eds. Ed Gillespie and Bob Schellhas (New York: Random House, 1994).
17. Carroll, *Annotated Alice*, 157.
18. Ibid.
19. Ibid., 161.
20. Ibid.
21. Ibid.

PART TWO

"THAT'S LOGIC"

"SIX IMPOSSIBLE THINGS BEFORE BREAKFAST"

George A. Dunn and Brian McDonald

Alice is a no-nonsense girl. Not that she's unadventurous or unimaginative. Far from it! And she's certainly not averse to taking advantage of the opportunities for fun afforded her by the magical worlds she encounters down the rabbit-hole and through the looking glass. But through it all, she displays a relentless insistence on making *sense* of things that continually runs afoul of the equally relentless insistence of the Wonderland and Looking-Glass worlds on making *nonsense* of everything. The mad chatter of the creatures that populate these worlds supplies much of the whimsy of Lewis Carroll's stories. But it's the maddening tug-of-war between Alice's obstinate good sense and the brilliant nonsense of the creatures she meets that supplies the hilarity.

"Everything Is So Out-of-the-Way Down Here"

Alice's forays down the rabbit-hole and behind the looking glass pit her in a two-front war against what we might call *tolerable* and *intolerable* nonsense. Most easily tolerated by Alice are the very things that would unhinge most of us in no time flat, the nonsensical conditions of these strange worlds with their surprising natural laws that decree, for instance, that edibles and drinkables are apt to instigate sudden and drastic changes in shape. What makes these bizarre conditions tolerable—even curiously stimulating—is that they can be mastered with a little trial and error. As the shape-changing rules get "curiouser and curiouser," they arouse Alice's own curiosity. Proceeding with a laudable—if somewhat reckless—willingness to experiment, she eventually discovers the useful properties of Wonderland mushrooms and can henceforth negotiate her new environment as a master of the rules of shape-changing rather than their helpless victim, nibbling one side or the other of the mushroom to produce whatever height she desires.

So when it comes to the curious *conditions* of Wonderland, Alice's efforts to make sense of the nonsensical pay off with dividends. But that's because the nonsense is only provisional, only on the surface, beneath which a diligent investigator like Alice is able to discover perfectly intelligible, albeit unexpected, laws of cause and effect. "One side will make you grow taller, and the other side will make you grow shorter,"[1] remarks the caterpillar about the rule that governs mushroom ingestion in Wonderland. People we know have reported some pretty spectacular results from eating mushrooms, but few as spectacular as that! As surprising as this outcome may be, though, it obeys the rules of Wonderland, and once Alice has learned what these rules are, she can count on them to operate as dependably as any of the laws of nature that obtain in our world. They only seem nonsensical to *us* because our experience in our world *aboveground* and *on this side of the looking glass* has burdened us with a slew of preconceptions about what can and cannot be accomplished by ingesting the caps of gilled fungi.

Our ordinary preconceptions about the effects of mushrooms—and, more generally, about what's really possible and impossible in our world—usually stand us in good stead, especially when they generalize from the actual experience of large numbers of people. They help make our world more manageable and trustworthy by allowing us to predict with confidence the likely outcomes of our actions and the course of events in the world, if not with infallible certainty, then at least well enough for most of our purposes. But in the extraordinary domains Alice discovers, governed by surprisingly different natural laws than those of our familiar world, her ordinary preconceptions about what's possible and impossible may actually impede her discovery of successful strategies for coping with the bizarre situations she encounters. Wanting to catch up with the Red Queen in the Looking-Glass world, Alice initially brushes off the advice of the Rose to walk in the opposite direction.

> This sounded nonsense to Alice, so she said nothing, but set off at once toward the Red Queen. To her surprise she lost sight of her in a moment, and found herself walking in the front door again.[2]

Walking in the direction opposite to where you want to go would indeed be nonsense on *this* side of the looking glass. But when Alice takes off in the direction that makes sense to her, she doesn't meet up with the Queen but instead runs smack into a reality that doesn't kowtow to her expectations. Immediately upon making this discovery, however, "she thought she would try the plan, this time, of walking in the opposite direction. It succeeded beautifully."[3]

It is to Alice's credit that she doesn't hesitate for a moment to discard her preconceptions when she comes across situations that patently refute them. In so doing, she displays an admirable readiness to encounter reality on its own terms, a receptive cast of mind that many philosophers would include among the most important "intellectual virtues" or character traits that assist us in the discovery of truth. (Alas, as we'll see shortly, this virtue is often in short supply among some of those who profess an interest in truth.) Coming upon a mouse, Alice wonders whether it might be fruitful to attempt to initiate a conversation with the creature and concludes, "Everything is so out-of-the-way down here, that I should think it very likely that it can talk: at any rate, there's no harm in trying."[4] She conducts the experiment, and to no one's great surprise, it succeeds.

"Very Few Things Indeed Were Really Impossible"

Alice's willingness to experiment is the fruit of her discovery that things in the Wonderland and Looking-Glass worlds don't necessarily obey the rules of our world. "So many out-of-the-way things had happened lately," we're told, "that Alice had begun to think that very few things indeed were really impossible."[5] She's absolutely right, too, provided that what she has in mind is what philosophers call *logical* possibility and impossibility. Philosophers often distinguish things that are logically impossible (for example, a *square circle*) from other things that people ordinarily judge to be impossible but are really just so "out-of-the-way" that most of us can't bring ourselves to believe that something like that would ever happen. Most of us would be extremely skeptical upon hearing a report that someone had witnessed a human infant changing by degrees into a pig, simply because that's not the sort of thing that normally occurs in our experience. But it *does* happen in Wonderland (to Alice's great consternation) and so, for reasons we're about to explain, we must conclude that such a horrifying (and hopefully rare) occurrence is at least logically possible.

Of course, it's reasonable to wonder how we can draw conclusions about what's possible and impossible *in general* on the basis of what happens in Wonderland, since this world of garrulous mice and grotesque metamorphoses exists only in the imagination. But that's precisely the point! Whatever can be imagined to be the case, however strange or out-of-the-way it might be, is logically possible. There are some things, however, that we simply can't imagine regardless of how hard we try, since they're inherently contradictory or nonsensical. Try imagining a *square circle*, for instance, or a *married bachelor*! You can't do it—not because of some shortcoming on your part, but because what you're being asked to imagine is denoted by a combination of words (*square circle*, *married bachelor*) that are literally nonsensical. Unless we make some wholesale changes to the ordinary meanings of these words (taking our cues from Humpty Dumpty, who, as we'll see shortly, believes he can make a word mean whatever he chooses), we all know that a figure can't be both a square and a circle at the same time, nor can someone be at once a bachelor and married. These and other unimaginable occurrences are among the "few things" that Alice rightly judges to be "really impossible."

There are, however, many other things that we improperly judge to be impossible for no other reason than that they don't conform to our established ideas about how the world normally goes, things that fall into the category that the philosopher David Hume (1711–1776) labeled *matters of fact*. *Matters of fact* constitute one of two categories into which Hume sorted the things about which people make enquiries and exercise their reason. The other category is *relations of ideas*. *Relations of ideas* pertain to the truths of mathematics ("Two plus three equals five."), pure logic ("Ferrets are ferrets."), and "every affirmation that is either intuitively or demonstrably certain."[6] Because the negation of any true statement of this sort is impossible—it's unimaginable, for instance, that two plus three could add up to anything but five—we know they must be true regardless of which side of the looking glass we may happen to be on. Moreover, we know that they're true not from experience or observation, but from "the mere operation of thought, without dependence on what is anywhere existent in the universe."[7] But *matters of fact*, which concern what actually goes on in the world, are a different story altogether. "The contrary of every matter of fact is still possible," observed Hume, since it's not inconceivable that the world could have been radically different than it is. Whether infants can turn into pigs—or, for that matter, whether one species can over the course of countless millennia gradually evolve into another—are questions that can't be answered through some peremptory judgment about what we believe is possible or not, but only through an investigation of how the world actually works, preferably conducted by someone who's "burning with curiosity" as intensely as Alice.[8]

Alice's curiosity, like her willingness to discard disproved preconceptions, is an important intellectual virtue, albeit one that in her case probably needs to be tempered on occasion with greater exercise of caution. Checking for a label marked POISON might be a good initial precaution before drinking the contents of an unknown bottle, for instance, but even in the absence of such an overt tip-off it's probably unwise to trust every bottle that turns up with an invitation to DRINK ME. Alice, however, is a trusting girl—and there's a way in which her trusting disposition can also be counted as one of her no-nonsense intellectual virtues. Alice has a fundamental trust that her efforts to understand reality, even the topsy-turvy reality of the worlds underground and behind the looking glass, will be rewarded. Even when things are behaving in the most unexpected manner, she always proceeds on the assumption that she can with effort make sense of them. No matter how astonishing the world she has fallen into may be, it is still a world in which reason reigns, even if sometimes in ways that are, as Alice puts it, decidedly "out-of-the-way."

"One Can't Believe Impossible Things"

So much for the *tolerable* nonsense, the nonsensical *conditions* of Wonderland and the Looking-Glass world that Alice can master with a little help from her ample store of intellectual virtues. Armed with a bold curiosity that never fails to keep pace with the "curiouser and curiouser" circumstances against which it's matched, a resolute faith in reason, and a fearless willingness to experiment and to discard disproved assumptions, our no-nonsense heroine regularly comes out the winner on this front of her war against nonsense. But there's another variety of nonsense that Alice is continually stumbling across in her adventures—the nonsensical *thinking* of the creatures that inhabit the worlds underground and behind the looking glass—and against their *intolerable* nonsense Alice never seems to be able to win because they use a strange form of logic to come to conclusions that are wholly irrational.

In a famous essay, "The Ethics of Elfland," G. K. Chesterton (1874–1936), a writer of fantasy and detective fiction who sometimes moonlighted as a philosopher, observed that there is a big difference between the wondrous and the irrational.

> You cannot imagine two and one not making three. But you can easily imagine trees not growing fruit; you can imagine them growing golden candlesticks or tigers hanging on by the tail. . . . We have always in our fairy tales kept this sharp distinction between the science of mental relations, in which there really are laws, and the science of physical facts, in which there are no laws, but only weird repetitions.[9]

As David Hume had pointed out over a century earlier, we've become so accustomed to certain regularities in nature that we sometimes mistakenly suppose them to be part of the necessary and unalterable fabric of reality as such. According to Chesterton, one of the most important lessons we can take from our sojourns in what he called Elfland, the realm of fantasy literature, is an appreciation of the non-necessity or inherent wondrousness of these regularities.[10] It's one of Alice's virtues that she doesn't fall prey to the error of thinking that any *matter of fact* is necessary. Consequently, she's able to experiment and discover some of the peculiar rules of her new environment, such as those that govern shape-shifting and locomotion, and come out a winner in her dealings with them. But the *arguments* that go on in these curious worlds are something she never can win—because the creatures are constantly asserting, in one form or another, that two and one equals something other than three!

"But one can't believe impossible things," cries Alice during a particularly frustrating encounter with the White Queen. The Queen, like modern purveyors of the efficacy of positive thinking, counters that all it takes is a little effort: "Why, sometimes I've believed as many as six impossible things before breakfast."[11] What stumps Alice here is that the statement is not *wholly* irrational. After all, generally, speaking, you *can* do a thing if you try hard enough! The statement hides its absurd content inside a general truth of observation.

Earlier in this encounter, the Queen uses another kind of logic, formal grammatical consistency, to make the impossible possible when Alice wonders when it will be "jam day."

> "The rule is, jam to-morrow and jam yesterday—but never jam *to-day*."
>
> "It *must* come sometimes to 'jam to-day,'" Alice objected.
>
> "No, it can't," said the Queen. "It's jam every *other* day: to-day isn't any *other* day, you know."
>
> "I don't understand you," said Alice. "It's dreadfully confusing!"[12]

It *is* dreadfully confusing, but it doesn't happen only in Wonderland and on the far side of the looking glass.

Philosophers who read Alice recognize that she is by no means the first to be victimized by the use of a specious logic. In fact, the logic of Wonderland has a long real-life history in philosophy. The great Greek philosopher Socrates (469–399 BCE), famous for saying, "The unexamined life is not worth living for a human being,"[13] had to contend with a clique of self-proclaimed savants calling themselves Sophists, who were notorious for using logic precisely to *prevent* such examination in favor of cleverly demonstrating how you *could* believe in six impossible things—before or after breakfast! The Sophists took their name from the Greek word *sophia*, meaning "wisdom," to advertise their claim to be *wise men*, but to many who listened to their arguments, *wiseass* seemed like a more fitting sobriquet.

In the *Euthydemus* Plato (427–347 BCE), who recorded many of Socrates' dialogues with his contemporaries, recounts how Socrates and some of his young friends are drawn into a conversation with two such Sophists—the brothers Euthydemus and Dionysodorus—who treat them to a cavalcade of arguments that rival those of the Wonderland and Looking-Glass creatures in absurdity. They confuse Socrates' young friend Cleinias as dreadfully as their counterparts do Alice, goading him through fallacious reasoning to consider—if not in the end believe—considerably more than six impossible things!

For example, Euthydemus asks Cleinias, "Which are the men who learn, the wise or the ignorant?"[14] Somewhat hesitantly, Cleinias responds, "the wise." Immediately, Euthydemus asks him a series of questions, the point of which is to show that since the act of learning presupposed being unlearned, those who learn are not the wise. But Cleinias has no sooner granted this seemingly reasonable inference than Dionysodorus jumps in to prove the exact opposite. He gets Cleinias to admit that when the grammar master gives dictation, it's the wise and not the unlearned boys that learn the dictation. The previous conclusion must have been wrong. Thus two apparently incompatible statements have been proven to be true. Impossible! And with such logic, the two men go on to "prove" many more impossible things, such as that *both* the unknowing and those who know learn, that Socrates' wish for Cleinias to be wise is a wish for him to "perish" (because he no longer wishes him to be what he was), that it's not possible to tell a lie, that no one has ever contradicted anyone, and so on.

Socrates is able to refute some of these *sophisms*, as such fallacious arguments have come to be called in honor—an admittedly *dubious* honor—of the Sophists who employed them with panache. Sometimes he's able to locate the precise point where the argument goes astray through some apparently valid but actually illicit inference. But often he just stands back from the arguments themselves in order to appraise their worth from the no-nonsense perspective of ordinary, levelheaded common sense: Euthydemus and Dionysodorus must be jesting, their arguments in the end refute themselves, or they amount to inconsequential quibbles over words. After all, you don't need to be a practiced logician to know that something has gone seriously wrong with an argument that purports to prove, as one of Dionysodorus's does, that it's impossible ever to make a mistake. "Look at it this way," Socrates advises the two Sophists:

> if it is impossible to speak falsely, or to think falsely, or to be ignorant, then there is no possibility of making a mistake when a man does anything? . . . If no one of us makes mistakes either in actions or in words—if this is really the case—what in heaven's name do you two come here to teach?[15]

What indeed! Obviously, the Sophists can't claim to teach us anything significant about the real world, that is, about matters of fact, since their own arguments supposedly demonstrate that each of us is already an infallible expert on everything.

Of course, we know this claim is absurd because experience is continually informing us that many of our beliefs about the world not only *can be* but frequently *are* mistaken. In fact, this recognition of the possibility of error, coupled with an earnest desire to get things right, is at the heart of the intellectual virtues exhibited by both Socrates and Alice when (each in his or her own way) they expose their thinking to the test of reality. By contrast, the Sophists use reason and logic in ways that are calculated to ensure that nothing can ever force them to admit error, in effect walling themselves off from reality rather than facilitating a fruitful encounter with it. But, as becomes apparent in the *Euthydemus*, the point of sophistical argument isn't to arrive at the truth in any case. It is, to use another term derived from the Greek, *eristic*, designed to defeat one's opponent at argument, without regard for the intrinsic merits or even the truth of the conclusion for which one is arguing.

Short on virtue but long on verbiage, the Sophists of ancient Greece have a great deal in common with many of the more loquacious creatures Alice meets in her adventures. Not only that, but Alice herself emerges as a kind of Socratic heroine who (both literally and figuratively) towers above those sophistic pygmies in her insistence on using reason to discover truth rather than exploiting the resources of a purely formal logic to reduce the world to a lot of self-willed nonsense.

"There's a Nice Knock-Down Argument for You!"

In Jefferson Airplane's famous song "White Rabbit," the acid-throated (and acid-taking) rock singer Grace Slick belts out a line describing Wonderland as the place "where logic and proportion haven fallen sloppy dead."[16] She's wrong. Logic, of a sort, is alive and well in the worlds Alice visits. It's proportion that's dead and gone. The creatures Alice meets aren't mad because they've lost their ability to perform operations of formal logic. They're mad because they've lost all sense of proportion, all sense of how matters of fact actually fit together and how reason can be used to shed light on them. They never use logic as a tool for understanding their world, as Alice does when she figures out how much "left-hand" and "right-hand" mushroom to eat in order to stay the right size. As with Euthydemus and Dionysodorus, these creatures use logic to *overthrow* the reasonable and justify wholly arbitrary conclusions.

This logical perversion is illustrated beautifully in the incident already discussed, in which the White Queen tells Alice she couldn't have jam today because the rule is "Jam every *other* day: today isn't any other day, you know." Logic is used here to wall off reality rather than to open it up for further understanding. The Queen is declaring that the perfectly possible is actually impossible!

And this approach can serve equally well to make the impossible possible. When the Cheshire Cat's unattached head floats about the croquet party, the King is annoyed and wants to get rid of it. The Queen's solution is her usual: "Off with its head." The executioner summoned to carry out the beheading argues quite reasonably "that you couldn't cut off a head unless there was a body to cut it off from," and the King retorts quite "logically" that "anything that had a head could be beheaded," adding "that you weren't to talk nonsense."[17] But, of course, it's the king who's talking nonsense here, sounding like Euthydemus and Dionysodorus, by taking a generally true observation, making it absolute, and then forcing it to fit a particular situation where it obviously doesn't apply. He's used an arbitrary logic that takes no account of the facts to "prove" the impossible to be possible.

Eristic logic turns its back on the intellectual virtue of honest inquiry and uses thought to fend off reality and paper over facts rather than open them up for exploration. The eristic motive of getting the better of an opponent in argument is nowhere more apparent than in Alice's run-in with Humpty Dumpty, who displays his eristic—even somewhat cantankerous—temperament in the following exchange:

> "Why do you sit out here all alone?" asked Alice, not wishing to begin an argument.
>
> "Why, because there's nobody with me!" cried Humpty Dumpty. "Did you think I didn't know the answer to *that?*"[18]

Alice may not have wished to begin an argument, but Humpty clearly has other plans. He seizes her innocent question as an opportunity to claim victory in what he insists on treating as the opening round of a verbal joust. Of course, his answer is perfectly sound, reminiscent of the old riddle, "Why did the chicken cross the road?" The answer: "To get to the other side." The humor in both cases lies in the fact that the answers to both questions are perfectly logical but not in the least bit informative. Neither is really an attempt to answer the question that was being asked. Attention is paid not to the question's meaning, but only to the form in which it was put. The logic may be perfectly sound, but the sense of proportion is "sloppy dead."

We confront this disjunction of meaning and form again in the following dialogue:

> "Here's a question for you," announces Humpty Dumpty. "How old did you say you were?"
>
> Alice made a short calculation, and said: "Seven years and six months."
>
> "Wrong!" Humpty Dumpty exclaimed triumphantly. "You never said a word like it!"
>
> "I thought you meant 'How old *are* you?'" Alice explained.
>
> "If I'd meant that, I'd have said it," said Humpty Dumpty.[19]

Connotation, a word's meaning in actual speech, is often different from *denotation*, the literal dictionary definition. In fact, phrases and whole sentences can have connotations quite distinct from their denotations. So honest dialogue partners look for the former and not the latter, as Alice is doing when she tells Humpty that she thought he meant "How old *are* you?" Humpty Dumpty, however, goes literal and denotative and thus wins. His triumphant exclamation is highly significant, leaving no doubt that triumph and not truth is his goal. The full implications of that emerge in the next triumphant battle of words.

Here Humpty Dumpty changes tactics. He has "won" the previous two exchanges by restricting the meaning of words and phrases to the literal or denotative, but he will now release them from any fixed meaning at all! He has just explained to Alice why "unbirthday" presents are better than birthday presents—because they increase the number of days on which you might get presents. At this point Humpty's logic has come at least within hailing distance of normal logic, but this will change as Alice challenges his conclusion that "there's glory for you!"

> "I don't know what you mean by 'glory,'" Alice said.
>
> Humpty Dumpty smiled contemptuously. "Of course you don't—till I tell you. I meant 'there's a nice knock-down argument for you!'"
>
> "But 'glory' doesn't mean 'a nice knock-down argument,'" Alice objected.
>
> "When I use a word," Humpty Dumpty said in rather a scornful tone, "it means just what I choose it to mean—neither more nor less."
>
> "The question is," said Alice, "whether you *can* make words mean different things."
>
> "The question is," said Humpty Dumpty, "which is to be master—that's all."[20]

That's one question. Another question is: How is it that in his prior exchanges with Alice, Humpty had enforced an absurd restriction of the meaning of words to the absolutely literal, but now he suddenly sees fit to indulge in a fantastic expansion of a word's meaning so that it can signify anything he pleases? Where these extremes meet is in the intention behind them, which has never been to discover the real meaning of what's being said, let alone the facts about the things in the world to which our words refer, but only to exercise a kind of sham mastery. It's all a sham, of course, for while such linguistic dexterity may aid Humpty in constructing what passes in the Looking-Glass world for "a knock-down argument," it can never bring you one whit closer to discovering the truth.

"Consider Your Verdict!"

This treatment of words as objects of mastery rather than tools for discovery governs a lot of what goes on in Wonderland—and, come to think of it, in the real world as well, where political discourse and social reality so often take the form of the famous trial of the Knave of Hearts for his alleged theft of the tarts. The King of Hearts' attempt to have the jury "Consider your verdict"[21] before any evidence has been given and the Queen's demand, "Sentence first, verdict afterwards,"[22] may be amusing nonsense in Wonderland, but reality has often tragically imitated art in the famous show trials of Stalin's regime or, closer to home, the frequent convictions of African Americans on trumped-up charges.

So it isn't really necessary to follow Alice underground or through the looking glass to encounter the abundance of lunatic logic and an absence of intellectual virtue she found there. Turn on your TV to any cable news network and you're likely to see the sentence-first approach of the Wonderland trial on full display. Chances are that at the moment you're reading this, some Republican strategist and Democratic strategist are debating one of the hot-button issues of the day. They each know the position they're going to take even before they begin to examine the evidence or engage in reasoning—and so do you! Their arguments will be dictated by a predetermined verdict, not the other way around. It's always conclusion first, evidence and argument second, as opposed to true dialogue, where the direction runs the other way. Because of this prior commitment to a certain conclusion, each combatant—and that's precisely what they are!—will be able to construct arguments that are for all practical purposes as irrefutable as Humpty Dumpty's.

It would all sound very familiar to Alice.

NOTES

1. Lewis Carroll, *The Annotated Alice: Alice's Adventures in Wonderland and Through the Looking-Glass* (New York: Clarkson N. Potter, Inc., 1960), 73.
2. Ibid., 205.
3. Ibid.
4. Ibid., 41.
5. Ibid., 30.
6. David Hume, *An Enquiry Concerning Human Understanding: And Other Writings* (New York: Cambridge University Press, 2007), 28.
7. Ibid., 28.
8. Carroll, *The Annotated Alice*, 26.
9. G. K. Chesterton, *Orthodoxy* (Chicago: Moody Publishers, 2009), 78–79.
10. And let's face it—some of the regularities that have been discovered to obtain in our world are no less astounding than those that occur in Elfland or Wonderland, such as light bending when it passes by large objects and employees always tending to get promoted to their level of incompetence.
11. Carroll, *The Annotated Alice*, 251.
12. Ibid., 207.
13. Socrates declaimed this sentiment as a defense of his way of life at his trial in 399 BCE for impiety and corrupting youth. See *Four Texts on Socrates: Plato's Euthyphro, Apology and Crito and Aristophanes' Clouds*,

translated by Thomas G. West and Grace Starry West (Ithaca: Cornell University Press, 1998), 92 (38a).

14. Plato, *Euthydemus*, trans. Kent Sprague (Indianapolis: Hackett Publishing Company, 1993), 9 (275d).

15. Ibid., 30 (287a).

16. "White Rabbit," written by Grace Slick (Copperpenny Music).

17. Carroll, *The Annotated Alice*, 117.

18. Ibid., 263.

19. Ibid., 265.

20. Ibid., 268–269.

21. Ibid., 146.

22. Ibid., 161.

REASONING DOWN
THE RABBIT-HOLE:
LOGICAL LESSONS
IN WONDERLAND

David S. Brown

When Alice fell down the rabbit-hole, did reason and logic go with her? G. K. Chesterton once claimed that "Wonderland is a country populated by insane mathematicians."[1] Yet he also claimed that "Fairyland is nothing but the sunny country of common sense."[2] I believe Chesterton is right in seeing confusion in Wonderland but also in seeing common sense there as well. Lewis Carroll (as I will refer to Charles Dodgson) was a mathematician, a logician, and a teacher. In addition to writing two books on logic for a general audience—*Symbolic Logic* and *The Game of Logic*[3]—he also invented and discussed several logical paradoxes. I believe we can see Carroll as both teacher and logician in Alice's adventures, and that there are lessons in logic for us to discover in Wonderland.[4]

Let's begin with a definition of logic. Carroll wrote *The Game of Logic* to both educate and entertain children, but he sees logic as different from the skills developed in other games. This is because the student of logic "may apply his skill to any and every subject of human thought; in every one of them it will help him to get *clear* ideas, to make *orderly* arrangement of his knowledge, and more important than all, to detect and unravel the *fallacies* he will meet with in every subject he may interest himself in."[5]

So the business of logic is about (1) having clear ideas, (2) putting them into an orderly arrangement, and (3) identifying and dismantling fallacies (mistakes in reasoning that often confuse us). But, of course, Wonderland is full of confusion. How, then, can we expect to find logic there?

A Confusion about Collisions

It would be easy to see Alice's confusion throughout her travels as the result of Wonderland itself: its being nonsensical and illogical. But, as we shall see, this would be a mistake. Certainly, Alice finds herself in a strange new world, and, much like every other child, she tries to make sense of things as best she can. Indeed, we find ourselves just as puzzled as she is. We very quickly learn, though, that we can't take it for granted that this lower world will conform to our expectations.

The philosopher David Hume (1711–1776) once invited his readers to consider a situation not all that dissimilar to the one faced by Alice. "We [might] fancy," he says, that we were "brought on a sudden" into a world in which we couldn't be sure that "that one Billiard-ball would communicate motion to another upon impulse"[6] until *after* the fact. So much for Friday night at the pool hall! Such a world would be disturbing at best. In similar fashion, we are shocked and dismayed upon entering Wonderland. Alice's world contradicts our experience and expectations. Is Wonderland therefore misconceived? Hume would reject that outlook. We see one billiard ball strike another, and we expect to see the second ball move.

High school physics taught us that force is transferred in the collision, but Hume shakes our confidence:

> [M]ay I not conceive, that a hundred different events might as well follow from that cause? May not both of these balls remain at absolute rest? May not the first ball return in a straight line, or leap off from the second in any line or direction? All these suppositions are consistent and conceivable. Why then should we give the preference to one, which is no more consistent or conceivable than the rest? All our reasonings *a priori* [that is, in advance] will never be able to show us any foundation for this preference.[7]

This is just the sort of imagination needed to gain access to Chesterton's fairyland: "You cannot *imagine* two and one not making three. But you can easily imagine trees not growing fruit; you can imagine them growing golden candlesticks or tigers hanging on by the tail."[8] In the world of Reason, perhaps, things are certain and cannot be conceived of otherwise. Alas, however, everything else is up for grabs.

How, then, do we learn about the way a world works, whether ours or Wonderland? As Hume tells us, *"Causes and effects are discoverable, not by reason, but by experience."*[9] It turns out that this is how both Alice and the rest of us learn about the world into which we have been thrust. We learn by experience, by observation, and by the testimony of others. It is the job of logic to help "make orderly arrangement" of these things.

The Land of Logic

> "I know what you're thinking about," said Tweedledum; "but it isn't so, nohow."
>
> "Contrariwise," continued Tweedledee, "if it was so, it might be; and if it were so, it would be; but as it isn't, it ain't. That's logic."[10]

According to the philosopher Graham Priest (1948–), "What Tweedledee is doing—at least in Carroll's parody—is reasoning. And that, as he says, is what logic is about."[11] Aristotle (384–322 BCE), the founder of logic, gave us the most basic requirement of reasoning in the Law of Non-Contradiction: "The same thing cannot at the same time both belong and not belong to the same object and in the same respect."[12] If animals speak, then they can speak. If Alice is falling down a rabbit-hole, then she is falling. If she can't get into the garden because she is too big to fit through the door, then she is too big to fit through the door. The most basic rule of logic, therefore, is that we avoid contradictions.

But we must also avoid fallacies: those mistakes in reasoning that more times than not get us into a muddle. As Peter Alexander notes, "[T]he mere committing of logical fallacies is not usually comic," but "Lewis Carroll successfully used a system in which logical 'fallacies', the bases of so many of his jokes, could be funny."[13] Alexander sees a similar thread in the comedy of the Marx Brothers. For example, in the movie *A Day at the Races* (1937),

> Groucho, a horse-doctor, feels Harpo's pulse and says "Either he's dead or my watch has stopped." This can be considered as the conclusion of an argument like this—
>
> If he is dead I won't be able to time his pulse.
> If my watch has stopped, I won't be able to time his pulse.
> I cannot time his pulse.
> Therefore, either he's dead or my watch has stopped.[14]

Remember, logic is about making an orderly arrangement of clear ideas and avoiding fallacies. So let's take a look at some examples. I hope they will be enough to convince you that there are logical lessons to be learned even in

Wonderland—lessons that help us think better in "any and every subject of human thought."

Humpty Dumpty and the New Atheists

Our first duty, if we are to be good thinkers, is to get some clear ideas in our heads. You have to start somewhere. This means that we must be very careful about the assumptions we make, and very picky about the meanings of the words we use. So the first rule of good thinking is:

1. Be Aware of Your Assumptions

> "How am I to get in?" asked Alice again, in a louder tone.
> "*Are* you to get in at all?" said the Footman. "That's the first question, you know."[15]

Sometimes we don't begin at the beginning. Alice, in the passage just quoted, simply assumes that her desire to get in is appropriate, and then sets about to satisfying it. But assumptions can cause us a world of trouble. For example, in the trial of the Knave accused of stealing tarts, in which a supposedly incriminating letter is introduced as evidence, we see just how much trouble assumptions can cause:

> "If you didn't sign it," said the King, "that only makes the matter worse. You *must* have meant some mischief, or else you'd have signed your name like an honest man."[16]

Here the King simply *assumes* the Knave wrote the letter, and then tries to infer on top of that a sinister motive, which he then uses to prove the Knave's guilt as a tart thief. This flagrantly bad piece of reasoning convinces the Queen, but not Alice. When you assume what you are trying to prove you are not reasoning well, even though you may succeed in getting someone's head cut off.

2. Know What Your Words Mean

"I don't know what you mean by 'glory,'" Alice said.

Humpty Dumpty smiled contemptuously. "Of course you don't—till I tell you. I meant 'there's a nice knock-down argument for you!'"

"But 'glory' doesn't mean 'a nice knock-down argument,'" Alice objected.

"When *I* use a word," Humpty Dumpty said, in rather a scornful tone, "it means just what I choose it to mean—neither more nor less."

"The question is," said Alice, "whether you *can* make words mean different things."

"The question is," said Humpty Dumpty, "which is to be master—that's all."[17]

The philosopher Peter Geach (1916–) thinks that definitions, like the one Humpty gives to "glory," are "harmless so long as the new arbitrarily conferred meaning is far enough away from the old meaning."[18] But Antony Flew takes a harder line:

To do what Humpty Dumpty did and what too many real people also do is not merely to speak "very absurdly." It is also to act in bad faith. For to express oneself in a public language is to undertake to speak and ask to be understood in accordance with the established meaning conventions of that language.[19]

Interestingly enough, this is precisely what John Haught (1942–) claims the New Atheists (Richard Dawkins [1941–], Daniel Dennett [1942–], Christopher Hitchens [1949–], and Sam Harris [1967–]) are doing when they define "faith" as "belief without evidence"—scarcely how such medieval luminaries as Augustine, Anselm, and Aquinas would have defined it.[20] The New Atheists may define "faith" as they please. But it's no doubt a sign of *bad* faith to then use that caricature as a stick with which to beat the theologians. Surely we want better reasoning than that.

Why Nobody Ain't a Nobody

Now having some crisp and clear ideas to work with is great, but it won't guarantee you clear thinking any more than that fresh new two-by-four in your driveway gets you a fence. You've got a lot of work ahead of you; you actually have to build the fence. And you have to build arguments as well; they don't just self-assemble upon adding water—not even in Wonderland. There must be some sort of orderly arrangement of our ideas; things have to go in their proper places. Otherwise, we'll never make any headway in the world of ideas. So we'll also need some assembly instructions.

3. Don't Confuse Categories

"I see nobody on the road," said Alice.

"I only wish *I* had such eyes," the King remarked in a fretful tone. "To be able to see Nobody! And at that distance too! Why, it's as much as *I* can do to see real people, by this light!"[21]

Aristotle once claimed that assigning things to their proper categories—whether quantity, quality, time, or place—is essential for making sense of the world. We cannot ask, "Which is bigger or longer, a mile or a minute?" because there is no common measure by which to compare them. They are in different categories: one is a matter of quantity, the other of time. Similarly, we cannot say that the city of New York weighs seven pounds, though it is perfectly correct to inform a fellow traveler that New York isn't located in London. If your mail gets put in the wrong box, you don't get it. If your idea gets put in the wrong "box," none of us "gets it."

If you were simply listening to the conversation between the King and Alice, you would hear "nobody" and "Nobody" as the same thing. As readers, we have the advantage of seeing the difference, which dispels the confusion. Alice is using "nobody" as a quantifier, telling us *how many* bodies are on the road (none); by contrast, the King is using "Nobody" as a proper name to refer to *a person*. Now, a person isn't a quantity; not many people are these days. So Alice and the King are talking right past each other.

We can see this same mistake when Alice speaks of the category of *time*, while the Mad Hatter thinks she is talking about a person whose name is "Time":

> Alice sighed wearily. "I think you might do something better with the time," she said, "than waste it in asking riddles that have no answers."
>
> "If you know Time as well as I do," said the Hatter, "you wouldn't talk about wasting *it*. It's *him*."
>
> "I don't know what you mean," said Alice.
>
> "Of course you don't!" the Hatter said, tossing his head contemptuously. "I dare say you never even spoke to Time!"
>
> "Perhaps not," Alice cautiously replied; "but I know I have to beat time when I learn music."
>
> "Ah! That accounts for it," said the Hatter. "He won't stand beating."[22]

Abbott and Costello made this kind of error famous in their hilarious "Who's on first?" routine. (Watch it on YouTube and count the number of times they make this mistake.)

4. Don't Confuse Subjects and Predicates

> "Then you should say what you mean," the March Hare went on.
>
> "I do," Alice hastily replied; "at least—at least I mean what I say—that's the same thing, you know."
>
> "Not the same thing a bit!" said the Hatter. "You might just as well say that 'I see what I eat' is the same thing as 'I eat what I see'!"[23]

Here we have a different sort of problem, a problem reminiscent of the oft-repeated fundamentalist argument for the Bible alone being inspired. The Bible, so the argument goes, teaches that "All Scripture is that-which-is-inspired" (2 Timothy 3:16). We then get the conclusion that "All that-which-is-inspired is Scripture."[24] But in neither our world nor Wonderland does this pass as good reasoning. All horses may be four-legged things, but not all four-legged things are horses. Subjects and predicates can't be automatically (and safely) switched.

Green Eggs and Hammers

Try putting up a fence with an egg, or try eating eggs with a hammer. We often hear that everyone's opinion is just as good as anyone else's. In logic, nothing could be further from the truth. You can really blow it, and embarrass yourself big-time in the process. While there are an almost unlimited number of ways reasoning can go wrong, here's a tip to avoid one of the most common mistakes (fallacies).

5. Don't Confuse Sufficient and Necessary Conditions

> "I'm sure I'm not Ada," she said, "for her hair goes in such long ringlets, and mine doesn't go in ringlets at all; and I'm sure I can't be Mabel, for I know all sorts of things, and she, oh, she knows such a very little."[25]

Alice knows that Ada's hair has long ringlets and that Mabel knows very little. Knowing that a girl is Ada is therefore sufficient for knowing that that girl has long ringlets in her hair. Knowing that a girl is Mabel is sufficient for knowing that that girl knows very little. We can use hammers and eggs to understand more about sufficient and necessary conditions.

Hitting an egg with a hammer is a sufficient condition for having a broken egg—what else would I need to do to break it? A broken egg is what I get when I hit an egg with a hammer, so a broken egg is a necessary condition of hitting an egg with a hammer—I am assuming a normal hammer and egg, of course.

Because there can be more than one sufficient condition for breaking an egg (I might have used my hand, for example), I can't conclude that a broken egg proves I used a hammer. (Take another look at the quote from the Marx Brothers and see if you can find both examples of this error.) I also can't conclude that if I don't use a hammer, I won't have a broken egg (since I am clumsy and might have just dropped it). The reason these conclusions don't follow is that we cannot confuse sufficient and necessary conditions.

We can see examples of this kind of reasoning in the previous passage about Ada and Mabel. Alice is making two arguments here. The first goes as follows:

> If I am Ada, then I would have my hair in long ringlets.
> I do not have my hair in long ringlets.
> Therefore, I am not Ada.

This is the second:

> If I am Mabel, then I would know very little.
> I know all sorts of things.
> Therefore, I am not Mabel.

Both arguments have the same form; they differ only in the terms being used. In both, the necessary condition is being denied ("If I hit an egg with a hammer, I will have a broken egg"; "*I don't have a broken egg*"; "Therefore, I did not hit the egg with a hammer."). Here Alice is reasoning well.

But she goes on, trying to remember all sorts of things she knows in order to prove she is not Mabel. She can't remember her multiplication tables or geography, and she concludes that "I must have been changed for Mabel!"[26] This argument is similar to the ones above, with the exception that it is most certainly not a good way to reason. Her new argument goes like is:

> If I am Mabel, then I would know very little.
> I know very little.
> Therefore, I am Mabel.

Alice's reasoning here has gone seriously wrong. She is not denying the necessary condition, as she did above. Alice is instead affirming the necessary condition, and this gets her into all sorts of personal identity trouble. Can we conclude from a broken egg that it must have been hit with a hammer? Of course not, but this is very like what Alice has done.

A similar confusion of necessary and sufficient conditions can be seen in the natural sciences. A traditional view is that science tests hypotheses by experiments that can prove them true (or correct). If we want to know whether a hypothesis is true, we derive some prediction that we can test from it—the ability to make such a testable prediction has long been considered a way of distinguishing evolutionary science from, say, biblical creationism. A successful test(s) is then said to prove the hypothesis. But as Karl Popper (1902–1994) points out, while an unsuccessful prediction can prove a hypothesis wrong, a successful prediction cannot prove it right.[27] You might as well argue that because we have a broken egg, it must have been a hammer that did it. This is not the way of true philosophy.

The Lasting Legacy of Logic

I hope this brief account convinces you that there is logic in Wonderland and lessons to be learned, that reading Alice isn't just for children. I challenge you to read the work again and discover more of Carroll's lessons in logic there. There are no better words of encouragement that I can give you for studying logic than Carroll's own:

> It will give you clearness of thought—the ability to *see your way* through a puzzle—the habit of arranging your ideas in an orderly and get-at-able form—and, more valuable than all, the power to detect *fallacies*, and to tear to pieces the flimsy illogical arguments, which you will so continually encounter in books, newspapers, in speeches, and even in sermons, and which so easily delude those who have never taken the trouble to master this fascinating Art. *Try it*. That is all I ask of you![28]

NOTES

1. G. K. Chesterton, "A Defense of Nonsense," in *The Defendant* (London: J. M. Dent & Sons, Ltd., 1901), 66.
2. G. K. Chesterton, "The Ethics of Elfland," in *The Collected Works of G. K. Chesterton, Vol. I: Heretics, Orthodoxy, The Blatchford Controversies*, ed. David Dooley (Fort Collins, CO: Ignatius Press, 1986), 253. All subsequent references to Chesterton will be from this source.
3. Both reprinted by Dover Publications as *Mathematical Recreations of Lewis Carroll: Symbolic Logic and the Game of Logic* (New York: Dover, 1958). A second part of a planned three-part work on *Symbolic Logic* was being finished at the time of Carroll's death. It has been published in *Lewis Carroll's Symbolic Logic*, ed. William Warren Bartley, III (New York: Clarkson N. Potter, Inc., 1977). References to Carroll's *Logic* will be to this latter edition.
4. For an excellent account of this, see Robin Wilson's *Lewis Carroll in Numberland: His Fantastical Mathematical Logical Life* (New York: W. W. Norton & Company, Inc., 2008).
5. Carroll, *Logic*, 46.
6. David Hume, *An Enquiry Concerning Human Understanding*, ed. Tom L. Beauchamp (Oxford: Oxford University Press, 1999), 4.1.8, 28. Citations of this work will include section, part, paragraph number, and a page number to this edition.
7. Ibid., 4.1.10, 111.

8. Chesterton, "The Ethics of Elfland," 254.

9. Hume, *Enquiry*, 4.1.7, 110.

10. Lewis Carroll, *The Annotated Alice: Alice's Adventures in Wonderland and Through the Looking-Glass*, introduction and notes by Martin Gardner (New York: W. W. Norton & Company, 2000), 181. Graham Priest begins his *Logic: A Very Short Introduction* (Oxford: Oxford University Press, 2000) with this quote.

11. Priest, *Logic*, 1.

12. *Metaphysics* 1005b19, quoted from *Aristotle Selected Works*, 3rd edition, trans. Hippocrates G. Apostle and Lloyd P. Gerson (Grinnell, IA: The Peripatetic Press, 1991), 366.

13. See his "Logic and the Humour of Lewis Carroll,"*Proceedings of the Leeds Philosophical and Literary Society* 6 (1951): 556.

14. Alexander, "Logic and the Humour of Lewis Carroll," 565.

15. Carroll, *The Annotated Alice*, 59.

16. Ibid., 121.

17. Ibid., 213.

18. Peter Geach, *Reason and Argument* (Berkeley and Los Angeles: University of California Press, 1976), 42.

19. Antony Flew, *How to Think Straight: An Introduction to Critical Reasoning*, 2nd edition (New York: Prometheus Books, 1998), 88.

20. John Haught, *God and the New Atheism: A Critical Response to Dawkins, Harris, and Hitchens* (Louisville and London: Westminster John Knox Press, 2008), 4–5. Haught's point is also made by Terry Eagleton and John Lennox, among others.

21. Carroll, *The Annotated Alice*, 222–223.

22. Ibid., 72.

23. Ibid., 70–71.

24. Ron Rhodes makes this argument in *The 10 Most Important Things You Can Say to a Catholic* (Eugene, OR: Harvest House Publishers, 2002), 21.

25. Carroll, *The Annotated Alice*, 23.

26. Ibid., 23.

27. On this point, see A. C. Grayling, *An Introduction to Philosophical Logic*, 3rd edition (Oxford: Blackwell, 1998), 7–9.

28. Carroll, *Logic*, 53.

THREE WAYS OF GETTING IT WRONG: INDUCTION IN WONDERLAND

Brendan Shea

Alice encounters three curious inductive problems in her struggles to understand and navigate Wonderland. The first arises when she attempts to predict what will happen in Wonderland based on what she has experienced outside Wonderland. In many cases, this proves difficult—she fails to predict that babies might turn into pigs or that a grin could survive without a cat. Alice's second problem involves her efforts to figure out the basic nature of Wonderland. So, for example, it is difficult for Alice to see how she could *prove* that her experiences were the result of her dreaming and not something else. The final problem is manifested by Alice's attempts to understand what the various residents of Wonderland mean when they speak to her. In Wonderland, "mock turtles" are real creatures and people go places with a "porpoise" (and not a purpose). All three of these problems concern Alice's attempts to infer information about unobserved events or objects from those she has observed. In philosophical terms, they all involve *induction*.

Induction, it turns out, is hugely important to our daily lives. Induction allows us to figure out which foods nourish and which poison; induction guides our conviction of criminals and pardoning of the innocent; induction is the basis of all scientific knowledge. Induction also provides our sole basis for understanding *language*. But the problem with induction, as Alice learns, is that one always risks being wrong. In Wonderland, many of Alice's inductively supported beliefs turn out suddenly to be false, and she is forced to start from scratch. Her successes and failures in doing so offer a window into the working of inductive reasoning, and should therefore be of real interest to us.

How to Avoid Poison and Red-Hot Pokers

Induction is a type of reasoning that stands in explicit contrast to *deduction*. In order to reason deductively from known facts to a conclusion, one must show that it is *impossible* for the conclusion to be false on the assumption that the original facts are as we thought. Lewis Carroll offers the following example of a deductive argument in his *Symbolic Logic*: "All cats understand French; some chickens are cats" therefore, "Some chickens understand French."[1] The conclusion is, of course, false. However, if one *assumes* that the first two statements are true, there is *no way* the third statement could be false. In using deduction, one never really goes beyond what one knows—one merely restates it in new (and sometimes interesting) ways.

In contrast to deductive reasoning, inductive reasoning attempts to go beyond what is already known. An inductive argument attempts to supply probable reasons for its conclusion. There are no guarantees. So, for example, were Alice to reason from *No rabbits have ever spoken to me before today* to the conclusion that *No rabbits will speak to me today*, she would be reasoning inductively. This is because, as Alice discovers, it is *possible* for the first statement to be true and the second false.

Most, if not all, of our everyday beliefs about the world have been arrived at by inductive reasoning. Alice provides a few good examples of inductively supported beliefs when she considers drinking the bottle labeled DRINK ME:

> It was all very well to say, "Drink me," but the wise little Alice was not going to do *that* in a hurry. "No, I'll look first," she said, "and see whether it's marked '*poison*' or not"; for she had read several nice stories about children who got burnt, and eaten up by wild beasts, and other unpleasant things, all because they *would* not remember the simple rules their friends had taught them: such as, that a red-hot poker will burn you if you hold it too long; and that, if you cut your finger *very* deeply it usually bleeds; and she had never forgotten that, if you drink much from a bottle marked "poison", it is almost certain to disagree with you, sooner or later.[2]

All of the rules Alice cites are good (if simple) ones. Nevertheless, we have only inductive reasoning to support them. For instance, the reason we think that fires will burn us in the future is because we know that they have burned us in the past. The same holds true any time we believe something on the authority of some reliable teacher, parent, or book. In fact, nearly all of our basic beliefs about history, science, and other people have been arrived at by inductive reasoning.

Why Predicting the Future Is a Problem

One common type of inductive reasoning involves our attempts to *predict* what we will experience in the future based on what has happened in the past. For example, most of us believe that rabbits will not begin talking, nor will babies suddenly become pigs. But suppose that somebody (we'll pretend it is Humpty

Dumpty) disagrees with us about these beliefs. Humpty claims that at 6:00 A.M. tomorrow the world we know will suddenly turn into Wonderland. Animals will talk, playing cards will hold trials, and people will change size dramatically when they eat certain foods. What, if anything, could we say to convince Humpty that he is wrong?

In his famous book *An Enquiry Concerning Human Understanding*, David Hume (1711–1776) argues that there is nothing we could say to *rationally* persuade someone like Humpty that he is wrong. Hume's argument proceeds as follows. First, he divides knowledge into two categories: that pertaining to *relations of ideas* and that pertaining to *matters of fact*.[3] Hume thinks that knowledge of the former category is possible, but it pertains only to truths we can figure by reflecting on the nature of our own ideas. For example, Hume thinks we can know that all triangles have three sides and that all bachelors are unmarried, but this knowledge doesn't depend on the *existence* of any triangles or bachelors. Even if every male in the world were married, for example, it would remain true that *if* there were a bachelor, he would be unmarried. This is guaranteed by our idea of bachelorhood. Hume might be quite happy with Humpty's observation that we are the "master" of our words.[4] According to Humpty's story, we can figure out whether "All triangles have three sides" is true or false simply by considering what we mean by words like "triangle."

In addition to our knowledge of relations of ideas, Hume grants that we can have knowledge about the matters of fact we have already *observed*. For example, we know that we have not up until now observed rabbits talking or playing cards holding trials. Hume's problem of prediction concerns the possibility of knowing about *unobserved* matters of fact. Humpty's challenge is just a more specific version of this problem. We have not yet observed what will happen at 6:00 a.m. tomorrow; Humpty challenges us to justify our belief that the world will not suddenly change into Wonderland.

The difficulty of Hume's problem becomes apparent when we consider how we might do this. When we defend claims about relations of ideas, we can appeal to what we can or cannot imagine as our test. So, for instance, it is impossible to imagine a non-three-sided triangle or a female bachelor. Therefore, triangles must be three-sided, and bachelors must be male. But Humpty's claim that the world will become Wonderland isn't impossible to imagine; in fact, we visualize Wonderland whenever we read Carroll's work. As Hume notes, we can imagine *any* matter of fact being different: "*That the sun will not rise tomorrow* is no less intelligible a proposition, and implies no more contradiction, than the affirmation, *that it will rise*."[5] Nor can we defend our prediction as we do our beliefs about matters of fact we have already observed. Our beliefs about observed matters of fact are based on what we have seen, smelled, touched, and tasted. We can't sense the future in this way.

According to Hume, the only reason we don't think that the world will radically change tomorrow is that it hasn't ever changed in this way *before*. In fact, Hume thinks all of our beliefs about unobserved matters rest on one key assumption—*that the future will resemble the past*. The problem is that this assumption is *itself* a belief about an unobserved matter of fact. Moreover, it is precisely what Humpty was asking us to defend. He agrees that up until today, the world has never radically changed. He just thinks that starting tomorrow, it will. And it seems we have no rational way of convincing him he is wrong.

Hume's conclusion is not that we have no basis for making predictions, but rather that our ability to do so successfully is quite independent of our deductive reasoning ability. Alice, for instance, shows little evidence of being an expert on deductive logic. However, she uses inductive reasoning with great success. In learning how to change her size by the consumption of various foods and drinks, for example, Alice is using inductive reasoning in order to make successful predictions. Her use of evidence about past events to predict and control the future course of nature is prototypical of scientific reasoning, and gives some idea of just how important prediction is to our everyday lives. Humpty Dumpty, who by contrast seems fairly competent at deductive logic, provides a good example of a poor inductive reasoner. When Alice first encounters Humpty, he is singing a song about how all the King's men won't be able to put him back together again. When queried by Alice, however, Humpty seems oblivious to the obvious predictive relevance of such a song, and refuses to move from his precarious perch. Humpty, despite his argumentative acumen, seems destined for a poor end.

Whose Dream Is This, Anyway?

From now on, let's suppose we've solved Hume's problem, and have managed to become perfect predictors. That is, let's suppose we're perfect at predicting what will happen to *us* in the future—what we will see, touch, taste, and smell for the rest of our lives. We now come to a new problem: What about our beliefs about things we *can't* sense in this way? Are they justified? Consider Alice's dilemma at the end of *Through the Looking-Glass*, when she is trying to determine whether her experiences were the result of *her* dream or whether they were the result of the *Red King's* dream. It seems obvious to us, of course, that it must have been Alice's dream. The problem for Alice, however, is to explain to a skeptic (like Tweedledee) *why* she is justified in believing that it is her dream.

Alice's problem is a special case of what the philosopher W. V. Quine (1908–2000) calls the problem of *underdetermination* of theory by evidence.[6] Here a person's *theory* is simply the collection of all of her beliefs about the world. Alice's theory, for instance, includes such beliefs as *London is located in*

England and *I am not a character in the Red King's dream.* By contrast, Tweedledee's competing theory includes the belief that *Alice is a character in the Red King's dream.* Someone's *evidence,* in Quine's sense, consists of everything that she can sense. Alice's evidence, for example, includes her memory of seeing the Red King sleeping and her memory of apparently "waking up." The problem, says Quine, is that no matter how much evidence we gather, there will always be multiple incompatible theories that can explain all of it.

Consider Alice's experience of waking up. This might seem to rule out Tweedledee's theory. After all, if Alice woke up, it must have been her dream, right? Tweedledee has an easy response, however. The reason that it seems to Alice that she is real and has woken up is because this is exactly what the Red King is dreaming. Tweedledee makes just this point when refuting Alice's claim that her tears show her reality: "I hope you don't suppose those are *real* tears."[7] In fact, it turns out there is no possible piece of evidence that Tweedledee cannot accommodate by making suitable changes elsewhere in his theory. On the basis of such considerations, Quine concludes that nearly any statement can be reconciled with any piece of evidence: "Any statement can be held true come what may, if we make drastic enough adjustments elsewhere in the system."[8] No amount of evidence-gathering, it appears, will allow Alice to prove Tweedledee wrong.

The relevance of underdetermination to everyday life becomes apparent when we note that Tweedledee's style of argument can be applied to challenge *any* belief we have about things that can't be directly sensed. And we have lots of those beliefs. Many scientific theories, for example, posit the existence of things too small or strange to be directly sensed: quarks, gamma rays, electrons, and gravitational forces. Scientists, using inductive reasoning, believe that these things exist because their existence explains the types of things we can examine with our senses. The problem of underdetermination states that there will always be some *other* theory (incompatible with ours) that could *also* explain this evidence.

It is not just scientists who believe in things they can't see. Alice, for example, believes that drinking the potion caused her to shrink and not the rest of the world to grow. However, there is nothing she could sense that would allow her to determine which process is actually happening. Alice, like the rest of us, also believes in object *permanence*. She believes that the Duchess she encounters at the Queen's party is the *same* Duchess she saw earlier. But this isn't the only theory that could explain Alice's experience. One might alternatively think that the world is being destroyed and instantaneously created anew each second. We don't remember any such destructions, of course, but that is only because we were created so as to have (false) memories of a continuous experience. According to this theory, Alice is in fact seeing a different Duchess than the one she remembers meeting. Once again, there is nothing Alice could ever do to discover whether such a theory was true or false.

Like Hume, Quine does not intend for his problem to induce skepticism about the value and legitimacy of scientific inquiry or our ordinary ways of doing things. Instead, he is merely pointing out that successful inductive reasoning requires more than (1) deductive reasoning or (2) making successful predictions. Quine goes on to suggest three criteria by which we decide which theories we adopt.[9] First, we need to make sure our theory doesn't contain false claims about our sensory experiences. Thus, Alice shouldn't adopt the theory that she's never had a Wonderland experience. Second, we should adopt theories that are as *simple* as possible. It's simpler, all things considered, to believe that there was only *one* Duchess instead of two. Finally, when we add new beliefs to our theory, we ought to change as *few* of our old beliefs as possible. If Alice were to believe that she were a character in the Red King's dream, for instance, she would have to change nearly every other belief she had (all of which presumed that she was real). The belief that the land beyond the looking glass was her own dream, in comparison, fits quite well with the rest of Alice's beliefs.

In the end, of course, there is no way of ensuring that one's theory is correct, just as there is no system for making perfect predictions. It might simply turn out that Alice and Tweedledee, even after comparing evidence, are both justified in their respective beliefs, despite these beliefs contradicting each other. The correct response to this, according to Quine, is simply to note that one *must* continue to believe in the truth of *some* theory; without it, one couldn't get around in the world. Alice's solution of recognizing the problem and simply going about her life is thus perfectly fine.

There's No Meaning in It, After All

Before considering the final problem, let's pretend that we've solved the first two. We're perfect at predicting what will happen to us, and we've come up with a complete, true theory of how the physical world works. The last problem of induction asks us to use this knowledge to determine what various people *mean* by their words. This is a source of constant frustration to Alice, who has to deal with such nonsensical characters as the Mad Hatter, the Queen of Hearts, and Humpty Dumpty. Almost every character in Wonderland and beyond the looking glass misuses or equivocates on some key English word or phrase, and Alice is tasked with using her inductive reasoning skills to figure out what is meant *in English* by such Wonderland words as "Time," "whiting," and so on.

Quine takes up the problem of determining what people mean by their words in a book called *Word and Object*. In order to simplify matters, he supposes that a hypothetical translator finds himself (like Alice) alone in an environment in which it is unclear what various people mean by their words.

The translator has no dictionary and no access to bilinguals who speak both English and the native language (which I'll call Wonderese). After a careful consideration of the process by which this translation might proceed, Quine concludes that there will always be multiple incompatible ways to translate Wonderese words into English; that is, it is *indeterminate* what people mean by their words. To see how he arrives at this strange conclusion, it will help to consider Alice's struggles in a little more detail.

The first step in any translation is to establish which native sounds mean *yes* and *no*. Alice herself notes the reason for this when she fails in her attempt to translate her kittens' sounds into English:

> It is a very inconvenient habit of kittens (Alice had once made the remark) that, whatever you say to them, they *always* purr. "If they would only purr for 'yes' and mew for 'no', or any rule of that sort," she had said, "so that one could keep up a conversation! But how *can* you talk with a person if they *always* say the same thing?"[10]

Once we have figured out which native sounds mean *yes* and *no*, we can ask the natives questions to determine what they mean by various other sounds. It is through this process that Alice discovers that "whiting" is the stuff used to polish shoes beneath the ocean and that "Time" is somebody that the Mad Hatter knows.

The problem arises, Quine observes, when one realizes that there will always be multiple English translations that can explain the answers Wonderland residents give to Alice's questions. So suppose that Alice is trying to figure out whether the Wonderese speakers mean the same thing she does by "rabbit." She first points to the White Rabbit and asks a group of them, "Rabbit"? They respond affirmatively. In order to be extra-careful, Alice points to the White Rabbit and his rabbit relatives at various times and places, and under all sorts of conditions. The Wonderland inhabitants continue to agree. However, Alice cannot establish that the Wonderese word "rabbit" means the same thing as the English word until she rules out the possibility that the Wonderland inhabitants are referring to something that is *co-located* with rabbits. Some things that are co-located with the White Rabbit, for example, are all of his various *parts* (arms, legs, and so on). Perhaps the Wonderese word "rabbit" refers only to some essential part of a rabbit (the heart, for example) when this part is attached to the rest of the rabbit. It is in this spirit that Quine writes, "Point to a rabbit and you have pointed to a stage of a rabbit, to an integral part of a rabbit, to the rabbit fusion, and to where rabbithood is manifested."[11]

The problem becomes even worse when one is trying to figure out the meanings of abstract words such as "intelligence," "courage," or "acceleration." The things these words refer to are quite difficult (nay, impossible) to point to. The Dormouse's question, "Did you ever see such a thing as a drawing of a muchness!"[12] might strike us as quite silly, but it presents a significant problem for Quine's translator. In the case of an expression such as "much of a muchness," there might be quite a number of sayings in other languages that could serve as adequate translations.

No doubt there are some limits on the translations we can adopt. In particular, we shouldn't adopt translations that get the natives' patterns of assent and dissent wrong. For example, Alice has good reasons not to translate the Wonderese "rabbit" as meaning *mouse*. The problem is: once we satisfy this minimal constraint, we have no grounds for convincing someone who has a *different* translation that she ought to adopt ours instead. Suppose that the Red Queen were to visit Wonderland with Alice. She would presumably try to come up with a translation that made the connections to her own language as simple (Looking-Glass-ish) and straightforward as possible, while Alice would try to do the same with English. Still, even after all the facts not related to meaning are settled, the translations might not agree.

In the real world, there are a variety of factors that keep us from disagreeing about translations of particular languages. It is very difficult, after all, to inductively reason our way to a translation based solely on our observations of native speakers. It is much easier to rely on dictionaries or textbooks, many of which are based on decades of careful research by linguists. In Wonderland, by contrast, this indeterminacy presents a much more obstinate and obvious problem. Wonderland residents repeatedly misunderstand both Alice and one another in strange (and sometimes malicious) ways. When Alice objects that the note in the Knave's trial means nothing, the King exclaims, "If there's no meaning in it that saves a world of trouble, you know, as we needn't try to find any,"[13] before launching into his own biased translation. Humpty Dumpty seems to have much the same philosophy when he offers Alice a translation of "Jabberwocky."

Not surprisingly, Alice's actions again suggest to us the best path to follow. In most cases, she strives to translate people's words in the way she would want her own words understood. If it seems crazy to Alice that people would mean a certain thing by a particular word, she usually assumes that they *don't* mean that until their actions prove her wrong. Her attempts to provide translations are thus based on her sense of *charity*. Alice presumes that other people agree with her on the types of things that she takes to be true. This assumption cannot be established by perfect prediction, nor by scientific investigation, but must be assumed as a starting point for translation.

Wonderland and the Real World

At the end of her adventures, Alice wakes up and returns to a world more similar to our own. It would be a mistake, however, to suppose that Alice need leave behind all she has learned about Wonderland, or that her experiences have nothing to teach us. Wonderland presents us with a weird sort of parallel Earth where our expectations fail us and we must figure out everything anew. In doing so, we come to see the importance of inductive reasoning for surviving our daily lives, for uncovering the nature of the world around us, and for understanding one another. These are projects that we, like Alice, cannot help but care about.

As readers, we can look to Alice for a model of what it takes to be a good inductive reasoner. Alice, unlike the strange creatures she encounters, learns to control her size, and does not fall prey to the fatalistic belief that she lives only in the dream of another. In contrast to the jurors in the Knave's trial, Alice realizes how preposterous the interpretation of the note really is. And she does all of this in the face of repeated challenges to her justification for reasoning as she does. In the end, Alice serves as a good reminder that not *all* reasoning is pointless or silly, and that a good reasoner is much more than an expert in the verbal gymnastics practiced by the residents of both Wonderland and our own world.

NOTES

1. Lewis Carroll, *Symbolic Logic* (London: Macmillan, 1896), 64.
2. Lewis Carroll, *The Annotated Alice: Alice's Adventures in Wonderland and Through the Looking-Glass*, ed. Martin Gardner (Bungay, UK: Penguin Books, 1965), 31. Subsequent references to the *Alice* stories are from this text.
3. David Hume, *An Enquiry Concerning Human Understanding*, 2nd edition, ed. Eric Steinberg (Indianapolis: Hackett Publishing Company, 1993), 14.
4. Carroll, *The Annotated Alice*, 269.
5. Hume, *Enquiry*, 15.
6. Quine discusses this problem in his book *Word and Object* (Cambridge, MA: MIT Press, 1960) and his famous paper "Two Dogmas of Empiricism," in *From a Logical Point of View* (Cambridge, MA: Harvard University Press, 1980), 20–47.

7. Carroll, *The Annotated Alice*, 239.
8. Quine, "Two Dogmas of Empiricism," 43.
9. Quine, *Word and Object*, 19–22.
10. Carroll, *The Annotated Alice*, 341.
11. Quine, *Word and Object*, 52–53.
12. Carroll, *The Annotated Alice*, 103.
13. Ibid., 159.

IS THERE SUCH A THING AS A LANGUAGE?

Daniel Whiting

"I Speaks English, Doesn't I?"[1]

"There is no such thing as a language." Who would say such a thing? The Mad Hatter? Humpty Dumpty? No, the remark is Donald Davidson's (1917–2003), one of the foremost philosophers of the twentieth century.[2] Such a remark is bound to raise eyebrows. Isn't Davidson using language in order to deny its existence? And isn't that precisely the sort of thing that reinforces the stereotype of philosophy as a non-subject that creates problems where there aren't any, and arrives at views one can't take seriously through some kind of intellectual trickery? But Davidson doesn't *just* say that there is no such thing as a language—he adds, "not if a language is anything like what many philosophers and linguists have supposed."[3] In other words, we should think of language *differently* from the way many do.

While it would be difficult to take philosophy seriously as an intellectual discipline if it involved nothing but making absurd (perhaps nonsensical) remarks, we don't mind that Lewis Carroll's novels involve an awful lot of this; on the contrary, we delight in it. But it would be a mistake to contrast too sharply the Alice novels with Davidson's writings. A main task of philosophy is to explore our capacity for making sense of things. It's principally via *language* that humans seek to make sense of their world and their place in it—and language is a preoccupation of the Alice novels. The meanings of expressions are repeatedly the topic of conversation. Characters endlessly explain, correct, and direct one another's utterances. ("'What do you mean by that?' said the Caterpillar sternly. 'Explain yourself!'"[4]) It should come as no surprise, then, that Carroll's work, like Davidson's, invites us to consider philosophical questions about the nature of language. But the affinities between Davidson's work and Carroll's don't stop there. The very considerations lying behind Davidson's Carrollesque remark are considerations the Alice novels explore.

"That's Not a Regular Rule: You Invented It Just Now"[5]

According to Davidson, many philosophers suppose that "speaking and writing are 'rule-governed' activities,"[6] and that the meanings of expressions are determined by these rules. For example, there might be rules according to which one should apply "red" only to things like *this* (pointing to a red sample), and one may make the transition from "This is red" to "This is colored" but not to "This is blue." Since this account sees language as a system of rules regulating behavior, I'll dub it *The Institutional View*. The view certainly has intuitive appeal. As Davidson notes, it promises to explain how we are able to learn languages and communicate with them by acquiring "the ability to operate in accord with a precise and specifiable set of . . . rules."[7] Nonetheless, Davidson thinks this view is mistaken. In conversation we often use "expressions not covered by prior learning" or "which cannot be interpreted" according to established rules. Yet the "hearer has no trouble understanding the speaker in the way the speaker intends."[8] Davidson offers his own examples, but Carroll gives us plenty to consider.

When falling down the rabbit-hole, Alice wonders if she'll reach "The Antipathies," though she's "rather glad there *was* no one listening, this time, as it didn't sound at all the right word."[9] Although "prior learning" alone won't help in understanding Alice's use of "antipathies," we *do* understand her; we know that she's wondering if she'll reach the Antipodes. Soon after, Alice is "opening out" like a telescope and cries, "Curiouser and curiouser!"[10] While Alice had "for the moment . . . quite forgot how to speak good English," we have no difficulty taking her to mean that her circumstances are becoming increasingly peculiar. Later, the Mock Turtle refers to "uglification":

"I never heard of 'Uglification,'" Alice ventured to say. "What is it?"

The Gryphon lifted up both its paws in surprise. "What! Never heard of uglifying!" it exclaimed. "You know what to beautify is, I suppose?"

"Yes," said Alice doubtfully: "it means—to—make—anything—prettier."

"Well, then," the Gryphon went on, "if you don't know what to uglify is, you *are* a simpleton."[11]

In this instance, Alice *is* being simple. Though the term "uglification" is novel, it takes little effort to ascertain what the Mock Turtle intends by it.

On occasions like this, we are able to converse despite the fact that some of the words being used are not "governed by learned conventions or regularities."[12] Thus, following shared rules, Davidson concludes, isn't *necessary* for communication. And, he claims, neither is it *sufficient*. For example, if a rule governs "antipathies," it doesn't enable us to understand Alice.

The prevalence of homophones—words pronounced the same but differing in meaning—also helps Davidson's case:

> "Mine is a long and a sad tale!" said the Mouse, turning to Alice, sighing.
> "It *is* a long tail, certainly," said Alice, looking down with wonder at the Mouse's tail; "but why do you call it sad?"[13]

Suppose that "tail" and "tale" are subject to rules of use; this doesn't allow Alice to understand the mouse; she needs in addition to grasp which meaning he intends.

Next, consider the fact that you and I might follow established rules for using words, but I still might not understand you if I can't see what you're getting at, if you don't convey your point of view. When the Hatter explains the workings of his watch, which "tells the day of the month, and doesn't tell what o'clock it is," Alice feels "dreadfully puzzled. The Hatter's remark seemed to have no sort of meaning in it, and yet it was certainly English."[14]

In light of such cases, Davidson concludes, what's required for communication, and all that's required, is *not* that we both use terms according to shared rules but that I attribute to your words the meanings that you *intend* them to bear. Davidson wants to replace the institutional view of language use—which emphasizes subjection and constraint—with one that registers the creativity and flexibility of language use, the need for imagination, enterprise, and innovation in order to achieve, via conversation, a meeting of minds. Let's call it *The Invention View*.

Since the Alice novels continually thwart our linguistic expectations and demonstrate the limitations of those expectations, we might take them to advance the invention view. It's certainly captured in the Duchess's injunction "Take care of the sense, and the sounds will take care of themselves,"[15] which suggests that what matters for communication is not the specific words uttered, but their being understood in the intended way. The Alice novels also mock the utility of "lessons," of the sort one finds in a "French lesson-book," when trying to converse with a mouse.[16] And we're surely not to take seriously the Red Queen's guidance on how Alice should speak—including, "Open your mouth a *little* wider when you speak"—whose result is that "For some minutes Alice stood without speaking."[17] Moreover, the shift from rules to intentions to communicate is echoed in the White King's complaint: "My dear! I really *must* get a thinner pencil. I can't manage this one a bit; it writes all manner of things that I don't intend—."[18]

Nonetheless, while the Alice novels certainly encourage us not to exaggerate the role rules play in communication, they also exhibit a sympathetic attitude to the institutional view. "If [cats] would only purr for 'yes,' and mew for 'no,' or any rule of that sort," says Alice after escaping the linguistic maelstrom of the looking glass, "so that one could keep up a conversation."[19] In a moment, we'll consider just where the Alice novels diverge from Davidson, but first let's take a look at another area of convergence.

"What's the Use of a Book without Pictures or Conversation?"[20]

"Success in communicating," Davidson insists, "is what we need to understand before we ask about the nature of meaning or of language."[21] The Alice novels agree. In *Wonderland*'s opening paragraph, Alice wonders what "use" is "a book without conversation."[22] And we're told that Alice "was very fond of pretending to be two people" when alone, suggesting that talking or giving "very good advice" to oneself is somehow parasitic upon talking to another.[23] Accordingly, when stuck in the Rabbit's house, Alice "went on, taking first one side and the other, and making quite a conversation of it altogether," at least until "she heard a voice outside."[24] Unsurprisingly, Alice feels "quite pleased to have got into a conversation" when she meets the Duchess,[25] and is equally "pleased to have somebody to talk to" when the Cheshire Cat appears.[26] Elsewhere, Alice has "conversations" with a mouse in a river of tears, a hookah-smoking caterpillar, and the Mad Hatter,[27] and pretends to converse with a kitten and a house.[28]

Behind this shared emphasis on communication is hostility to what I'll call *The Solipsist View*, according to which the nature of language can be understood by focusing on the individual speaker in isolation from her physical and social environment.[29] (A solipsist believes that only she exists.) Davidson's certainly no fan of the solipsist view, insisting as he does on "the essential social element in linguistic behaviour."[30] "We would not have a language," he claims, "if there were not others who understood us and whom we understood; and such mutual understanding requires a world shared both causally and conceptually."[31] We come across the solipsist view when the White Knight falls "headlong into a deep ditch":

> "How *can* you go on talking so quietly, head downwards?" Alice asked, as she dragged him out by the feet, and laid him in a heap on the bank.
>
> The Knight looked surprised at the question. "What does it matter where my body happens to be?" he said. "My mind goes on working all the same. In fact, the more head downwards I am, the more I keep inventing new things."[32]

For the Knight, where his "body happens to be"—which physical or social environment it's in—is irrelevant to his mind's "working" and its "quiet" expression in language. Indeed, the White Knight thinks that the further removed he is from conversation, the greater his capacity for "inventing." Given the absurdity of his inventions—including horse's anklets to "guard against the bites of sharks"[33]—we're evidently not supposed to endorse his perspective.

Davidson's hostility to the solipsist view drives his hostility to the institutional view. Interestingly, however, the Alice novels associate the solipsist with an *inventor*, suggesting that it's actually the invention view that suffers from lingering solipsism.

"There's a Nice Knock-Down Argument for You"[34]

At this point, you might be wondering whether *some* grasp of rules for language use isn't in fact necessary. For Davidson, grasp of rules is "a practical crutch to interpretation, a crutch we cannot in practice afford to do without—but a crutch which, under optimum conditions for communication—we can in the end throw away, and could in theory have done without from the start."[35] But what do the "optimum conditions" Davidson mentions involve? If they involve interlocutors having superhuman powers, it might be true that *in theory*, when such conditions obtain, participants in a conversation can do *without* rules. But giving weight to this seems at odds with the anti-solipsist insistence on keeping in view, when seeking to understand the nature of language, what is actually required for communication of the sort creatures like ourselves engage in, embedded in the kinds of circumstance we find ourselves in. So, assuming optimum conditions don't involve superhuman abilities, is grasp of rules unnecessary for communication? While "Sheer invention is . . . possible,"[36] it's surely *parasitic* upon established rules. One wouldn't understand what's being expressed in Alice's use of "curiouser" or the Mock Turtle's use of "uglification" without a prior understanding of terms such as "curious" and "beautify," and so arguably a grasp of the rules standardly governing their use. Likewise, being unfamiliar with the proper use of "Jabberwocky's" terms, Alice simply "couldn't make it out at all," needing Humpty Dumpty to explain that "'*Brillig*' means four o'clock in the afternoon."[37] In the absence of guidelines, it seems, communication cannot proceed.

By way of analogy, consider the Caucus-race, whose partic-ipants "began running when they liked, and left off when they liked,"[38] or the Queen of Heart's croquet game, in which there don't seem to be "any rules in particular; at least, if there are, nobody attends to them."[39] It seems that for an activity to be meaningful and purposive, some rules need to be opera-tive. (The dominant motifs of both novels are rule-governed activities: cards and chess.)

The invention view seems to assume that whether an utter-ance has meaning and what meaning it has is entirely up to the speaker. But this smacks of solipsism, as if understanding what you say is fixed wholly by your intentions—entirely indepen-dently of external influence. Humpty maintains such a view:

"There's glory for you!"

"I don't know what you mean by 'glory,'" Alice said.

Humpty Dumpty smiled contemptuously. "Of course you don't—till I tell you. I meant 'there's a nice knock-down argument for you!'"

"But 'glory' doesn't mean 'a nice knock-down argu-ment,'" Alice objected.

"When *I* use a word," Humpty Dumpty said in a rather scornful tone, "it means just what I choose it to mean—neither more nor less."

"The question is," said Alice, "whether you *can* make the words mean so many different things."

"The question is," said Humpty Dumpty, "which is to be master—that's all."[40]

This exchange makes clear that one can't simply mean by one's utterance what one chooses to mean, for meaning isn't entirely due to an isolated individual; it is influenced by exter-nal factors. Alice is not immune to Humpty's mistakes:

"Then you should say what you mean," the March Hare went on.

"I do," Alice hastily replied; "at least—at least I mean what I say—and that's the same thing, you know."

"Not the same thing a bit!" said the Hatter. "You might just as well say that 'I see what I eat' is the same thing as 'I eat what I see'!"[41]

Alice thinks that what one says is always what one intends to say, that what one gets across in communication coincides with what one intends.

Of course, Davidson agrees that Humpty's view is absurd. But he insists that what impose constraints are *not* common rules but *intentions to communicate*:

> In speaking or writing we intend to be understood. We cannot intend what we know to be impossible: people can only understand words they are somehow prepared in advance to understand. . . . Flying by the net of language could not, then, imply unrestrained invention of meaning.[42]

Davidson grants, then, that one doesn't create meaning "*ex nihilo*, but on the basis of our stock of common lore,"[43] which includes knowledge of past or typical uses of expressions. But, one wonders, if Davidson allows that communication usually requires sensitivity to patterns of usage, the ways expressions are regularly employed, what reasons are there for resisting the short step to allowing that communication usually requires sensitivity to rules that establish such patterns and regularities? It's hard to see any.

I've conceded ground to Davidson, accepting that appealing to shared rules is inadequate for explaining how communication proceeds. At most, I've shown that grasp of rules is sometimes required, not that it always is. However, it doesn't follow, as Davidson suggests, that the notion of linguistic rules is of no significance. Nothing so far said undermines the idea that grasp of rules could *possibly* (if not indispensably or alone) play a role in conversation, or that such rules *typically* facilitate and influence communicative exchange.

Consider that often what we *actually* express, and are taken to mean, when we utter words is at odds with what we *intend* to say. Alice is a victim of this several times. Indeed, although the Alice novels are often viewed as belonging to the genre of literary *nonsense*, it is striking how frequently characters take Alice *literally*, thinking she means just what her words mean. For example:

> "What is it you want to buy?" the Sheep said at last, looking up for a moment from her knitting.
>
> "I don't *quite* know yet," Alice said, very gently. "I should like to look all round me first, if I might."
>
> "You may look in front of you, and on both sides, if you like," said the Sheep: "but you can't look *all* round you—unless you've got eyes at the back of your head."[44]

Alice expresses herself in a way apt to mislead by not choosing words typically understood to express the thought she means to convey, namely *that she'd like to look around the shop first*. Of course, it's really the Sheep in the wrong, focusing too much on the words chosen and not enough on the purpose of the utterance, which makes Alice's intention clear. Clearly, however, some kind of established meaning *is* affecting the conversation, and it's certainly tempting to view that meaning as determined by rules. This situation, of what one's words (institutionally) mean influencing what one is taken to mean, is nicely captured in the Red Queen's moral: "When you've once said a thing, that fixes it, and you must take the consequences."[45]

Next, consider Alice's altercation with Humpty:

> "How old did you say you were?"
>
> Alice made a short calculation, and said, "Seven years and six months."
>
> "Wrong!" Humpty Dumpty exclaimed triumphantly. "You never said a word like it!"

"I thought you meant, 'How old *are* you?'" Alice explained.

"If I'd meant it, I'd have said it," said Humpty Dumpty.[46]

Or Alice's reply to the March Hare's offer of "more tea":

"I've had nothing yet," Alice replied in an offended tone, "so I can't take more."

"You mean you can't take *less*," said the Hatter: "it's very easy to take *more* than nothing."[47]

In these exchanges, Alice's understanding of the words of her conversational partners is at odds with what is literally expressed by them. Again, Alice is in the right, since in ordinary conversational contexts, unlike mad tea parties, one would understand an offer like the Hare's to imply that one's already had some tea.[48] The important point is that his words seem to bear a kind of established meaning that competent speakers are sensitive to, and that influences (if not fixes) what is implied. Again, it's tempting to view that meaning as determined by rules as opposed to a speaker's intentions on a given occasion.

So Davidson is right to suggest that grasp of shared rules is insufficient for communication, that "mutual understanding is achieved through the exercise of imagination, appeal to general knowledge of the world, and awareness of human interests and attitudes."[49] But he's not shown rules (and with them established meanings) to be entirely unnecessary for communication or to play no part whatsoever. There might be a role for the institutional view after all, albeit a more modest one.

Davidson might question whether we need to appeal specifically to rules in explaining what is going on in situations such as those above. One might view the established meaning as fixed, not by rules, but by the accumulated weight of past usage in communication, which subjects are familiar with, and which generates certain expectations and determines a range of ways in which the new utterance might be understood. But, again, if Davidson is prepared to allow this much, there seems little reason to stop short of accepting that rules do, as a matter of fact, play a wide-ranging role in communication, even if grasp of them isn't enough for communication to succeed, and even if there can be innovative occasions of communication that transcend the rules. Davidson unfairly saddles the institutional view with commitments it needn't bear. All that it need involve is the thought that there are rules for the use of words that determine their (literal) meanings, not that those rules always be shared or remain constant over time.

"Language Is Worth a Thousand Pounds a Word"[50]

Ultimately, Davidson is hostile to the institutional view because he associates it with the solipsist view. He thinks that it presents linguistic competence as involving a kind of "portable interpreting machine set to grind out the meaning of an arbitrary utterance,"[51] that it views communication as a matter of mechanically executing algorithmic commands without sensitivity to one's conversational partners and specific situation. But one can view language use as involving rules while insisting that interlocutors need in addition a degree of worldly wisdom, imagination, and sensitivity—an ability to tailor and even disregard rules as occasions demand. Moreover, by presenting conversations as if they arose out of nowhere, without the baggage of history and social circumstance, it appears that Davidson's invention view suffers from its own solipsism. The Alice novels remind us that it is simply a fact about us that we find ourselves flung into a world already containing certain institutions, including languages, which constrain, facilitate, and influence our behavior. Indeed, through initiation into rule-governed linguistic practices, subjects appropriate a sophisticated system of principles for forming and manipulating representations of the world, a system no isolated individual, or pair, could establish from scratch. Alice certainly appreciates the benefits of accumulated wisdom:

> She had read several nice little histories about children who had got burnt, and eaten up by wild beasts and other unpleasant things, all because they *would* not remember the simple rules their friends had taught them: such as, that a red-hot poker will burn you if you hold it too long; and that if you cut your finger *very* deeply with a knife, it usually bleeds; and she had never forgotten that, if you drink much from a bottle marked "poison," it is almost certain to disagree with you, sooner or later.[52]

So, Davidson gives us no reason to deny altogether the existence or importance of linguistic rules. Rules are not everything. But they're not nothing either. There *is* such a thing as a language, even if language is a lot like what many philosophers have supposed.[53]

NOTES

1. Lewis Carroll, *Through the Looking-Glass* (London: Penguin, 1994), 156.
2. Donald Davidson, *Truth, Language, and History* (Oxford: Oxford University Press, 2005), 107.
3. Ibid.
4. Lewis Carroll, *Alice's Adventures in Wonderland* (Harmondsworth, UK: Penguin, 1994), 54.
5. Ibid., 151.
6. Davidson, *Truth, Language, and History*, 152.
7. Ibid., 110.
8. Ibid., pp. 94–95, 90.
9. Carroll, *Alice's Adventures*, 14.
10. Ibid., 21.
11. Ibid., 115.
12. Davidson, *Truth, Language, and History*, 93.

13. Carroll, *Alice's Adventures*, 36.

14. Ibid., 83.

15. Ibid., 107.

16. Ibid., 28. "Lessons" are referred to repeatedly in both novels.

17. See Carroll, *Through the Looking-Glass*, 37–39, 44, 145–147, 160–162.

18. Ibid., 26.

19. Ibid., 170.

20. Carroll, *Wonderland*, 11.

21. Davidson, *Truth, Language, and History*, 120.

22. Carroll, *Alice's Adventures*, 11.

23. Ibid., 19.

24. Ibid., 44.

25. Ibid., 70.

26. Ibid., 100–102.

27. Ibid., 29, 53–54, 82.

28. Carroll, *Through the Looking-Glass*, 16, 31.

29. What I say here broaches a debate in philosophy of language and mind concerning whether what a subject says or thinks is determined in part by the physical or social environment she is in. For an opinionated route into this debate, see Gregory McCulloch's *The Mind and Its World* (London: Routledge, 1995).

30. Davidson, *Truth, Language, and History*, 109.

31. Ibid., 176.

32. Carroll, *Through the Looking-Glass*, 135–136.

33. Ibid., 130.

34. Ibid., 100

35. Donald Davidson, *Inquiries into Truth and Interpretation*, 2nd edition (Oxford: Oxford University Press, 2001), 279.

36. Davidson, *Truth, Language, and History*, 100.

37. Carroll, *Through the Looking-Glass*, 102.

38. Carroll, *Alice's Adventures*, 33–34.

39. Ibid., 99–100.

40. Carroll, *Through the Looking-Glass*, 100.

41. Carroll, *Alice's Adventures*, 82.

42. Davidson, *Truth, Language, and History*, 147.

43. Ibid., 157.

44. Carroll, *Through the Looking-Glass*, 86–87.

45. Ibid., 151.

46. Ibid., 97.

47. Carroll, *Alice's Adventures*, 88; see also *Through the Looking-Glass*, 97, 146–147.

48. Paul Grice, in *Studies in the Way of Words* (Cambridge, MA: Harvard University Press, 1989), investigates in detail the distinction between what an utterance literally expresses and what it implies given the conversational context. Grice's writings can be intimidating. For an accessible introduction, see William Lycan's *Philosophy of Language: A Contemporary Introduction*, 2nd edition (London: Routledge, 2008), ch. 13.
49. Davidson, *Truth, Language, and History*, 110.
50. Carroll, *Through the Looking-Glass*, 47.
51. Davidson, *Truth, Language, and History*, 107.
52. Carroll, *Alice's Adventures*, 17–18.
53. Many thanks to my wife, Hayley, and to my colleagues at Southampton for invaluable feedback on earlier incarnations of this material.

PART THREE

"WE'RE ALL MAD HERE"

ALICE, PERCEPTION, AND REALITY: JELL-O MISTAKEN FOR STONES

Robert Arp

When I was young, I loved the *Alice* stories, like any other kid. But now that I'm older, I can't help but think to myself: "What was this Lewis Carroll dude smoking when he wrote this?" I'm not alone, obviously, as numerous people have made this observation over the years. Being in a drug-induced state can cause someone to wonder if what they're perceiving is really what's going on in reality. I had a bizarre reaction to a pain-killer once when I was in the hospital. I thought someone had stacked stones for me to eat on the bedstand next to me. From my hallucinogenic perspective, the stones were there waiting to be eaten. I called the nurse in to ask her if she saw the stones, too, and after laughing a bit, she told me I was "seeing things" that were not there, probably from the pain-killer. It was actually Jell-O on my bedside stand.

The *Alice* story and my hallucinogenic hospital experience caused me to think about the difference between what I perceive to be the case and what really is the case concerning myself, the world around me, and reality in general. But what makes up a person's "reality"? Is reality just my own collection of perceptions and ideas, or is there a world outside of me? And if there is my world of perceptions and a world outside of me, then how, if at all, can I get beyond these perceptions to know if they match up with reality? Assuming that there is a reality beyond my perceptions, I want to be secure in my knowledge of that reality. I want to *know* that my perception of a pebble is in fact a pebble, and that my experience of Jell-O really is Jell-O. But how can I be secure in my knowledge?

The theme of appearance and reality emerges time and time again in the *Alice* stories. What Alice *perceives to be* the case is not always what *really is* the case. Consider that the whole Wonderland story itself is one huge dream, since Alice's sister wakes her up for tea at the end. Alice never really visited an actual place called Wonderland; she just thought she did. In this chapter, we'll explore this perception/reality distinction that can be found in the *Alice* stories. We'll begin by distinguishing between a perceiver, her perceptions, and the external objects she is perceiving. To help us understand how these things are related, we'll look at two important distinctions in metaphysics (the study of being itself) and epistemology (the study of human knowing). In the end, we'll see that both Alice and Lewis Carroll maintain that there is indeed a real world—our perceptions tell us as much.

"The Confused Clamor of the Busy Farm-Yard"

It seems obvious that other people, farm animals, rabbits, cats, decks of cards, even mathematical relations like the Pythagorean theorem, exist "out there" beyond our perceptions of them. Most of us take it for granted that there is a world of things existing outside of our minds, regardless of whether we are perceiving them or not. And in fact such things would continue to exist whether or not they were perceived by us or anyone.

Take a moment, however, to think about what you are aware of when you perceive other people, farm animals, rabbits, and the like. For example, right now I'm sitting at my computer typing this chapter on a deck overlooking a beach on Lake Michigan. I see the computer screen in front of me, I smell the lake water, I hear the waves crashing on the shore, I feel the tips of my fingers strike the keypad, and I feel the deck under my feet. I can also close my eyes and form an image or idea of the screen, keypad, deck, lake, and waves.

Notice that we can talk about three different kinds of things in this example:

1. **The Perceiver** There is me, the *perceiver* who has the perceptions and ideas.
2. **The Perception** There are *my perceptions* of the screen, keypad, deck, lake, and waves that take the forms of the

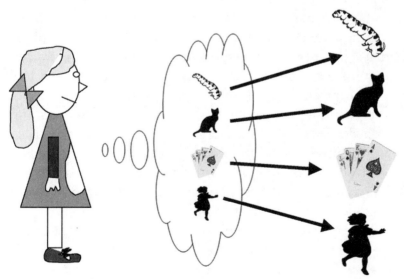

Alice the perceiver, Alice's perceptions, and Alice's perceived world.

sensations of sight, sound, and feeling, as well as images and ideas.

3. **The Perceived** There are the *external objects of my perception*, the actual computer and keypad sitting on the table, the lake itself, the hardwood deck.[1]

Consider the figure on page 127. There is Alice, who is the perceiver. There are Alice's perceptions, which include her sensations, thoughts, and ideas about caterpillars, cats, cards, and other things. Finally, there are the external objects of Alice's perceptions, which include actual caterpillars, cats, cards, and other things out there in the world.

"So She Sat On, with Closed Eyes, and Half Believed Herself in Wonderland"

But now certain questions arise. Can I really get beyond my own perceptions so as to have access to the screen, keypad, deck, lake, and waves *themselves* as they really are? Maybe all that I can perceive are my own perceptions? How can I be sure that the external objects of my perception are really there, or that how they present themselves to me in my perceptions matches up with or corresponds with how they really are? After all, I can't step outside of my own perceptions and look at myself in relationship to external objects to see if, in fact, my perceptions correspond with these external objects. Am I "locked inside" my own world of sense perceptions? If so, how do I even know that there is a world out there beyond my perceptions? This is at least part of how Alice probably feels at the end of her adventures when she wakes up on the riverbank and ponders what just happened.[2]

These questions and their surrounding issues have caused some thinkers to hold philosophical positions known as *epistemological idealism* and *metaphysical antirealism*. Epistemology is the area of philosophy concerned with the sources and justification of knowledge, and an epistemological idealist thinks that one's perceptions or ideas (thus, *idea*lism) are the only source of knowledge.[3] (I want to make it clear that I will be talking about *philosophical* idealism, which has nothing to do with the common understanding of idealism as referring to belief in ideal circumstances.) A possible consequence of this view is that I can never tell if my perceptions correspond with the external objects of my perception. The perceiver is forever barred from access to the objects of perception. Alice probably felt this on numerous occasions. You would, too, if pebbles were turning into cakes all around you.

Metaphysics is the area of philosophy concerned with the nature and principles of what really exists, and a metaphysical antirealist (of the hard-core variety) thinks that there is no real world outside of one's perceptions or ideas.[4] Idealism and antirealism fit together nicely. "After all," reasons the idealist, "all I can ever know are my own perceptions of things as they appear to me." In other words, my own perceptions make up or constitute *all of what I can know*. And "after all," reasons the antirealist, "if all I can ever know are my own perceptions of things as they appear to me, and I cannot get outside of myself to see if my perceptions match up with any reality, then my perceptions must be the sum total of my reality." In other words, my own perceptions make up or constitute *all of reality*. If I were Alice thrust into Wonderland, after a certain amount of time I would start to think like an antirealist!

Epistemological idealism and metaphysical antirealism can be contrasted with *epistemological realism* and *metaphysical realism*.[5] According to an epistemological realist, even though we have perceptions, there must be an outside world that our perceptions represent, for otherwise we would not have those perceptions in the first place. Despite the fact that the mind can be very creative in making up all kinds of ideas in the imagination, there seem to be certain perceptions and ideas that could not have been generated by the perceiver. In other words, there must be some things "out there" that directly cause the representation of our perceptions "in here."

For example, we can see how someone like Lewis Carroll can imagine all kinds of talking animals, grouchy cards, folk creatures, and mythological beasts. People have been doing this for as long as they have been telling stories. But how can the mind generate the idea of a fossilized fern, a dodo bird, or the Pythagorean theorem solely from its repertoire of perceptions and ideas? These things seem to have been *discoveries*, not invented constructions of the mind. In fact, Carroll was a bit of a mathematician, and people have pointed out the various mathematical references in the *Alice* story such as those related to circles, converse relationships, numerical limits, and bases. Again, it's hard to see that these mathematical objects—although understood, articulated, and explained by minds—were invented *solely* by minds.

This is where epistemological realism and metaphysical realism fit together nicely. If you believe that there is a world of things "out there" that really do exist and would continue to exist whether or not you or anyone perceive them, then you are a metaphysical realist. Consider that according to the theory of evolution, there was a time when human beings, complete with perceptions, did not exist. Are we to think, asks the realist, that prior to the evolution of the human mind, there was nothing occurring out there in the world? What are we to make of the fossilized fern? Was there no evolution taking place prior to our perceiving or thinking about the fern or any other fossil? This seems absurd. Didn't the fern exist and fossilize at some point prior to the existence of human minds and their perceptions? And wouldn't the fern have still existed and been fossilized, even if humans with minds to perceive things never existed? Dodo birds have not outlived our species, but other species likely will. Are we seriously to believe that these other species will cease to exist when we do?

Consider this Carrollesque twist on an old proverbial question: "If a caterpillar smoking a hookah falls off a mushroom in a forest and breaks his hookah, and no one is around to hear the hookah break, does it make a sound?" Sound requires a thing *to make* a noise as well as a thing *to hear* the noise. According to the realist, the hookah's crashing to the ground of the forest would produce sound waves whether there was anyone or anything around to perceive or pick up the sound waves. So technically, the hookah breaking would not make a sound if no one or no thing with the capacity to hear were present. But the breaking still would produce sound waves that could be picked up by a person or thing with a capacity for hearing sounds. On the other hand, the antirealist would have us believe that the hookah could crash to the ground without so much as a sound—that is, provided no one were around to hear it.

Further, realists believe that Pythagoras *discovered* and *formulated* the theorem that $a^2 + b^2 = c^2$ holds for a right triangle; Pythagoras didn't *wholly invent* it. Realists also believe that the theorem would exist and be what it is even if it were never discovered and formulated. In fact, realists believe that right now, out there in reality, there are all kinds of things waiting to be discovered by the human mind and its perceptions. Despite the fact that the mind can be quite creative in its imaginations, and despite the fact that there can be many different ways of perceiving, there is still some reality out there beyond the mind and its perceptions. To think that "reality" is constituted by the mind and its perceptions, as the antirealist does, is misguided, according to the realist.[6]

"All Would Change to Dull Reality"

Most people are epistemological and metaphysical realists, including Alice and Lewis Carroll. Despite the fact that Carroll's mind is full of all kinds of imaginary perceptions, he seems to take it for granted that his perceptions do, at times, accurately represent external objects. That the Wonderland story ends with Alice waking up from a dream state indicates to the reader that Carroll believes Alice, her sister, the river, the riverbank, and the tea are real objects of perception out there in the world (or at any rate, would be real objects if this were a true story, and of course real-world counterparts of the fictional entities are real). On the contrary, the Mad Hatter, the Queen of Hearts, Bill the Lizard, and other denizens of Wonderland are merely perceptions in various forms. Carroll has all changing "to dull reality" at the end of the story.

Alice is an epistemological and metaphysical realist, too. In the story itself, while she is actually experiencing Wonderland, there are moments when Alice can be mistaken about whether her perceptions represent external objects accurately, but she believes that her perceptions can still accurately represent external objects (insofar as there really are denizens of Wonderland). In fact, because Alice is aware of, and concerned with, the confusion, gross alterations, and crazy logic she perceives in herself, others, and the world of Wonderland, this shows that she thinks it is possible to have an accurate representation of external objects. The confusion, gross alterations, and crazy logic arise from a discrepancy in the relationship between her perceptions and the external objects of her perception existing in Wonderland.

Let's be careful here. Alice *thinks* or *believes* that there is a real world out there to be discovered, and she thinks that it can be accurately represented in her perceptions. Whether there is, in fact, an actual world out there is an open question. Obviously, Wonderland is not real! But it seems that Alice, like most of us, takes it for granted and just assumes that there is a real world beyond our perceptions. Alice combines her epistemological realism with her metaphysical realism. She thinks that it is possible for perceptions to represent external objects of perception accurately, and this is so because she believes that there is, in fact, a real world of external objects that exists whether perceived or not. When Alice is deceived by a person or thing presenting him or her or itself as someone/something other than who/what they are (for example, Alice claiming at the end of the story, "You're nothing but a pack of cards!"), she believes there is some real person or thing out there doing the deceiving.

"So She Was Considering, in Her Own Mind . . . "

One unfortunate consequence of holding to idealism and anti-realism is solipsism, from the Latin words *solus*, "alone" and *ipse*, "self." If all you are aware of is your own perceptions, and you are forever barred from knowing whether your perceptions match up with any external objects of your perception, then it would appear that you are alone in reality. It's as if you're "locked inside" your own world of perceptions, never knowing whether there is even any world out there beyond the perceptions.

This view is illustrated in the figure on page 134. Think of Alice as being locked inside the room of her own mind, kind of like someone trapped inside of a movie theater. Now imagine that there is a movie screen inside the theater, representing Alice's or anyone's perceptions, that is connected to a movie camera outside the theater that views the outside world. The camera represents a person's five senses. A perceiver, like Alice, only has access to her own perceptions on the movie screen of her mind. She could never get outside the room of her own mind to see if her perceptions match up with some external world, let alone whether such a world even exists![7]

We might respond that since life can be perceived to be solitary at some times but not at others, it cannot be a series of perceptions with no reality. For how would one know what a perception was if it were not for some reality with which it could be contrasted? Just as one could not understand what such things as pain, selfishness, or love were without a grasp of their corresponding opposites (pleasure, altruism, and hate),

Alice stuck in her own mind.

so, too, it seems that we couldn't even begin to understand what a perception was unless it were contrasted with reality. Consider that at the end of the story, the reader is led to believe that Alice's perceptions have been incorrect, that her adventures in Wonderland have been some sort of dream, and that she has now awakened once again to the real world, where she finds herself standing on the riverbank with her sister.

Perceptions Are Fine, but Dull Reality Is Still Better

The *Alice* stories fascinate us precisely because of the distinction between perception and reality. Our perceptions have enabled us to imagine all kinds of things and circumstances, and at times we all love to fantasize. We have all had dreams where we wish we would never wake up. But we have all had nightmares, too. When all is said and done, I'm glad that imagination, fantasies, and dreams are contrasted with reality because I prefer "dull" reality, as Carroll calls it. I can count on its reliable constants, and I never have to worry about talking rabbits! Yet, like Alice at the end of the story, I hope that we all go off at times to ponder all the curious happenings that make up the perceived and real worlds.

NOTES

1. In the history of Western philosophy, this three-part distinction can be traced back, at least, to Plato (427–347 BCE) in his famous work *Republic*, Book VII, where he talks about the allegory of the cave. In this allegory, Socrates asks his listeners to imagine someone (the perceiver) chained in a cave facing a wall. At first, the only things the person sees are shadows on a wall in front of him (the perceptions), which are produced as a result of things and people moving around behind him in the firelight (the external objects of perception). The person breaks free, turns around to see things in the firelight, and eventually makes his way out of the cave to see things clearly as they really are in the sunlight. The allegory is supposed to represent one's ascent from ignorance to knowledge, but it also can be viewed as a movement from perception to reality. Plato's *Republic* can be found in *The Collected Dialogues of Plato*, trans. Lane Cooper, eds. Edith Hamilton and Huntington Cairns (Princeton, NJ: Princeton University Press, 1961). For an excellent introduction to Plato's *Republic*, see Julia Annas, *An Introduction to Plato's Republic* (Oxford: Clarendon Press, 1981).

2. In the history of Western philosophy, distinguishing among me, my perceptions, and the external objects of perception became especially prominent for philosophers during the Modern period (ca. 1600–1800). The thinker usually looked to as the father of Modern philosophy, René Descartes (1596–1650), makes this distinction in his famous work entitled *Meditations on First Philosophy*. Other philosophers during this period, such as Leibniz, Spinoza, Locke, Berkeley, Hume, and Kant, are all concerned with the distinction and its implications for perception and reality. Important parts of these thinkers' works can be found in *Modern Philosophy: An Anthology of Primary Sources*, eds. Roger Ariew and Eric Watkins (Indianapolis, IN: Hackett Publishing, 1998). Also see the commentary in Garrett Thomson, *Bacon to Kant: An Introduction to Modern Philosophy* (New York: Waveland Press, 2001).

3. Good introductions to epistemology include Robert Audi, *Epistemology: A Contemporary Introduction*, 2nd edition (New York: Routledge, 2002), as well as Matthias Steup, *An Introduction to Contemporary Epistemology* (Upper Saddle River, NJ: Prentice Hall, 1995).
4. Good introductions to metaphysics include Michael J. Loux, *Metaphysics: A Contemporary Introduction*, 3rd edition (New York: Routledge, 2006), as well as Peter van Inwagen, *Metaphysics*, 3rd edition (Boulder, CO: Westview Press, 2008).
5. For discussions of epistemological and metaphysical realism, anti-realism, and idealism, see the articles in *Realism and Antirealism*, ed. William Alston (Ithaca, NY: Cornell University Press, 2002). Also see John McDowell, *Mind and World* (Cambridge, MA: Harvard University Press, 1994) and E. J. Lowe, *A Survey of Metaphysics* (Oxford: Oxford University Press, 2002).
6. For discussions of this sort, see Nicholas Rescher, *Objectivity: The Obligations of Impersonal Reason* (South Bend, IN: University of Notre Dame Press, 1997); also Robert Arp, "The Pragmatic Value of Frege's Platonism for the Pragmatist," *Journal of Speculative Philosophy* 19 (2005): 22–41.
7. In the history of Western philosophy, David Hume (1711–1776) figures prominently in suggesting the idea that the mind may be nothing other than a collection of perceptions, and that one may be considered a theater-goer, viewing the "perceptions successively making their appearance." See Hume's *A Treatise of Human Nature*, Section 4, parts of which can be found in *Modern Philosophy: An Anthology of Primary Sources*, eds. Roger Ariew and Eric Watkins (Indianapolis, IN: Hackett Publishing, 1998). Also, George Berkeley (1685–1753) seriously entertains the idea that we may be trapped inside our perceptual reality, with no access to the external world. He argues for such a position in *Three Dialogues between Hylas and Philonous*, significant parts of which are reprinted in Ariew and Watkins's anthology.

HOW DEEP DOES THE RABBIT-HOLE GO?: DRUGS AND DREAMS, PERCEPTION AND REALITY

Scott F. Parker

> "I imagine that right now you're feeling a bit like Alice. Tumbling down the rabbit-hole? . . . You take the blue pill and the story ends. You wake in your bed and believe whatever you want to believe. You take the red pill and you stay in Wonderland and I show you how deep the rabbit-hole goes."
>
> —Morpheus to Neo in *The Matrix*

Since its publication in 1865 *Alice in Wonderland* has become our defining cultural myth of distorted reality. We're all familiar with the characters (the Caterpillar, the Cheshire Cat, the Mad Hatter), the key phrases ("Off with their heads!"; "Curiouser and curiouser!"; "We're all mad here."), and the plot (Alice falls into a rabbit-hole, gets lost in Wonderland, and has a series of bizarre encounters as she tries to find her way home. Many of us also associate drugs, specifically hallucinogenic drugs, with *Alice*. Indeed, Alice's journey can be read as an allegory for an intense drug experience. Rephrasing the plot only slightly, Alice gets lost and tries to find her way back to *normal reality*. Within the story are specific allusions: the Caterpillar smokes a hookah, Alice drinks mysterious liquids and eats mushrooms, Alice's perceptions of time and space are altered, and the impossible is everyday. The association of drugs with *Alice* is so established that *alice* is now a slang term for LSD.[1]

But Is It a Drug Story?

Because *Alice* flavors drug use and depiction, there is an urge to retroactively read drug imagery into the story. For example, is it a coincidence that users *trip* on drugs and Alice goes on a *trip* to Wonderland, even sort of *tripping* to fall down the rabbit-hole? This is one way to go with an essay on *Alice in Wonderland* and drugs, to look for every possible allusion or depiction of drugs[2] and argue that the whole story is inspired by, a celebration of, or a guide to hallucinogenic drugs. If that's the sort of thing that interests you, it's a Google search away. For the purposes of this essay I'll use *Alice* as a guide to metaphysics (the study of reality) and epistemology (the study of knowledge), specifically the impact of drugs on perception and knowledge of reality.

The first big obstacle to thinking about the effect drugs have on Alice is that she doesn't actually ingest anything until *after* she has seen a talking rabbit, fallen down an almost bottomless pit at a comfortable speed, landed softly on the ground, and seen the same rabbit use a door, closing it behind him. In other words, Alice's world is already bizarre before she takes any drugs. This has to raise the question of whether we read too much into the story when we attribute the strangeness to drugs. Perhaps a literal reading is more appropriate: the story is a fantasy; the normal rules of the world are out the window; the "Drink Me" liquid, "Eat Me" cake, and mushroom do only what the narrator says, make Alice bigger or smaller. In a land as strange as Wonderland, this makes the drugs not all that special.

We learn at the end of the book that Alice has dreamed the whole story of Wonderland while sleeping under a tree avoiding her lessons. Reconsidering the story with this in mind, certain things make sense: the talking animals and playing cards, the importance of physical size (a pressing issue to a child who wishes she were older), the manifestation of Alice's desires (doors, magic potions), the dream-logic of the story (events beginning and ending abruptly in sync with the shifting attention of the dreamer). The revelation of the dream offers another viable reason for why normal rules are off, and looking at the perceptual and epistemological challenges of dreams will be the second main emphasis of this chapter.

Before we move on to philosophical analysis, let's examine a scene from *Through the Looking-Glass*, the sequel to *Alice in Wonderland*. In *Through the Looking-Glass*, Alice once again finds herself in a fantastical world, this time the other side of a looking glass. And once again we will learn that Alice has dreamed the whole thing up. In this dream, in chapter four of the novel, Tweedledee tells Alice the sleeping Red King is dreaming her into existence. The Alice in the story doesn't know that she's in a dream, and therefore doesn't think to ask if the real her, the one having the dream, is also being dreamed into existence, but we do know and we do ask. It's implied by analogy: If the Alice in the looking glass can be dreamed into existence by the Red King, can't the Alice in *Through the Looking-Glass*, who is dreaming of the other Alice and the King, be herself dreamed into existence by another being? The analogy is transparent to us. Lewis Carroll has dreamed up the Alice who dreams up the King who dreams up Alice. Except there's more. The character Alice was based on Alice

Liddell, a real girl Carroll knew and spent time with. The question then becomes, Who, if anyone or anything, dreamed up Liddell? And also, who dreamt Carroll? There's a kind of answer to this last: Charles Dodgson dreamed up Carroll as a pen name, but this just begs the question.

Anyone who's smoked a little pot will recognize this as classic drug thinking,[3] which is not necessarily to say it's bad thinking, just that it's inconclusive (like most philosophy?) and takes the metaphysical ground out from under the reader of *Alice*'s feet just as Wonderland and the looking glass take it out from under Alice's. We have a hard time saying much of anything substantive about the books, least of all the drugs, because everything is already called into question by the suspension of the normal rules of reality. It follows from this suspension that any connections between the story and the outside world are speculative and inconclusive. But there's at least one good reason that in the face of these epistemological obstacles we can do better than throw our hands up in defeat.

Life Is But a Dream?

Whether Alice is tripping or dreaming or actually in a fantastical world, her *experience* of reality is the same. She experiences it as if it is real. We know this as readers because her experience is given to us on the page and we have no reason to doubt the experience even as we might look for explanations of the causes of the experience. And so, as readers, we accept that Alice thinks she's, say, talking to a rabbit even if we don't think she's *really* talking to a rabbit. The difference between Alice's experience and our understanding of Alice's experience is much like the difference between accepting the story as a credulous child might and thinking about it critically. My main argument, as I've already hinted, is going to be that this distinction between a normal and distorted experience is exaggerated if not specious insofar as *normal* is suggestive of *real*. What *normal experience* actually means is not that we experience things as they are, but that we experience things as we normally experience things. We know that our experiences and perceptions are affected by expectations, weather, light, emotions, hormones, alertness, diet, exercise, personality, childhood trauma, and so on. This could be a very long list, to say nothing of drugs we may have ingested—prescription meds, nicotine, alcohol, caffeine, St. John's wort, Tylenol, and so on, another long list. It's not as if we see perfectly clearly until we dream or drink a mysterious liquid, at which point things go suddenly crazy. Objectively speaking, things already are crazy. And so, how do we trust our perceptions, whether awake or dreaming, sober or intoxicated?

Keeping in mind that our conceptions of *normal* and *distorted* are contingent on the way we habitually see things and that we have at best a weak claim to a *real* reality, let's look at the drugs and dreaming in *Alice in Wonderland* as paradigmatic cases of how reality—experience of reality—*changes*. The reasons I'm treating drugs and dreams so closely is that (1) they are so intermingled in *Alice*; and (2) in everyday life we act on the assumption that there is a clear demarcation between normal consciousness (lucid, waking thought) on the one hand and distorted consciousness (intoxication, dreaming) on the other.

Two philosophers who take on the problem of perception in a suitably Alice-like fashion are Plato and Chuang Tzu, each of whom writes about dreaming and self-identity. Plato, in *Theaetetus*, portrays a dialogue between Socrates and Theaetetus.

> Socrates: How can you determine whether at this moment we are sleeping, and all our thoughts are a dream; or whether we are awake, and talking to one another in the waking state?
>
> Theaetetus: I do not know how to prove the one any more than the other, for in both cases the facts precisely

correspond; and there is no difficulty in supposing that during all this discussion we have been talking to one another in a dream; and when in a dream we seem to be narrating dreams, the resemblance of the two states is quite astonishing.

Socrates: You see, then, that a doubt about the reality of sense is easily raised, since there may even be a doubt whether we are awake or in a dream.[4]

Compare those lines from Plato with these from *Alice*:

"But I don't want to go among mad people," Alice remarked.

"Oh, you can't help that," said the Cat: "we're all mad here. I'm mad. You're mad."

"How do you know I'm mad"? said Alice.

"You must be," said the Cat, "or you wouldn't have come here."[5]

The Cheshire Cat signals (to the knowing reader) that Alice is necessarily mad *because* she's in a dream. This could work for us as readers, but Alice lacks the privileged knowledge that we have (that she's dreaming), so to her the Cat's words come across as either wrong (she doesn't feel mad) or meaningless (how does he know?). And this is largely Plato's point in *Theaetetus*: neither in waking life nor dreaming life does one (usually) know with certainty which state one is in, and therefore we must be aware at all times of the *possibility* that we are mad.

A similar epistemological problem is raised in *Alice* when Alice meets the Caterpillar. She tells the Caterpillar, "Being so many different sizes in a day is very confusing." When he denies this, Alice goes on: "Well, perhaps you haven't found it so yet, but when you have to turn into a chrysalis—you will some day, you know—and then after that into a butterfly, I should think you'll feel it a littler queer, won't you?" Again the Caterpillar denies her. Now Alice makes a partial concession: "Well, perhaps *your* feelings may be different, all I know is, it would feel very queer to *me*."[6] This time, instead of denying Alice, the Caterpillar inquires directly into who is the Alice who would feel queer changing into a chrysalis and then a butterfly. This question of identity is interesting because it forces Alice to wonder: if she changes so much, is there a part of her that is the *real* Alice?

The ancient Chinese Taoist philosopher Chuang Tzu raises a similar butterfly question: "Once Chuang Chou dreamt he was a butterfly, a butterfly flitting and fluttering around, happy with himself and doing as he pleased. He didn't know he was Chuang Chou. Suddenly he woke up and there he was, solid and unmistakable Chuang Chou. But he didn't know if he was Chuang Chou who had dreamt he was a butterfly, or a butterfly dreaming he was Chuang Chou."[7] In terms of *Alice*, how does Alice know she's not a butterfly dreaming she's Alice, or a giant Alice dreaming she's a small Alice, or a different girl dreaming she's Alice, or so on? And then how do we know we're not butterflies dreaming we're human, or humans dreaming or hallucinating (for whatever reason)? Strictly speaking, we don't. We can't escape a measure of skepticism regarding our perceptions and identities, and yet we usually proceed as if our perceptions are reliable. And what do perceptions tell drug users, dreamers, and Alice, in addition to us in our normal waking hours? That *this* is real.

The Land of the *Real*?

"Remember all I'm offering is the truth."

—Morpheus to Neo, again, in *The Matrix*

"If the doors of perception were cleansed every thing would appear to man as it is, infinite."

—William Blake, *The Marriage of Heaven and Hell*

A number of people, and even a few philosophers, have claimed that the distortions from *normal* perception that drugs induce actually sometimes lead *to* a truer, realer understanding of reality, not *away* from it. This is a deeply counterintuitive position, because, as Bertrand Russell writes, "In the search for certainty, it is natural to begin with our present experiences, and in some sense, no doubt, knowledge is to be derived from them. But any statement as to what it is that our immediate experiences make us know is very likely to be wrong."[8] Such a statement would very likely be wrong because of the numerous imperfections with our perception: we see and hear only thin bands from the spectra of light and sound, and generally then only on scales that have been evolutionarily advantageous, and still with flaws.

But the argument that drugs can lead to a realer understanding of reality isn't that drugs improve perception. The position is actually that some drugs can sometimes precipitate a mystical experience, and in a mystical experience one sees the world as it truly is. Often this involves dissolving the separation between subject and object, and comes with an unflappable conviction that one is seeing things as they *really are*. The conundrum is that the mystic is sure that he sees how things really are but the experience is limited to himself. No one else can access it or verify it. But still, the mystic maintains, he's sure—or he was sure while he was in the mystical state.

As I've said, I'm skeptical of what it would even mean to *know* reality as such, and not *as* a human knowing it, except that I've had experiences that have *seemed more real* to me than my *normal* experience—and some of these experiences have been under the influence of drugs.

The first time I ate hallucinogenic mushrooms I went with some friends (also on psilocybin) to walk around the forest by the river near where we lived. I have no sense of how long we were there. Time was utterly irrelevant to me. I was so engrossed by my surroundings that I stopped thinking about anything that wasn't immediately present. My attention became increasingly focused until I was aware not of the forest but a pocket of it and eventually a single plant in the undergrowth. I studied the plant carefully, getting to know its movements and patterns. When I felt like I was really understanding the plant I looked down my arm to my fingers, which had been caressing the leaves, to find that I couldn't tell where my fingers left off and the leaves began. My hands and the plant's branches were connected quite seamlessly and naturally. Now, a few things were going on. Visually and tactilely, there was no separation between the plant and me, but at the same time part of me knew that my arm wasn't a plant and that it just seemed that way because of the mushrooms. And yet I was grateful because I knew I was learning something, viscerally instead of abstractly, about the way I was connected to my environment. While I'm disinclined to trust the hallucination completely, the insight was certain and remains with me in a diluted form to this day. That it sounds kind of silly now I take as proof of the ineffability of the insight, not as a failure of the insight itself.

I'm not sure how much to read into this—isn't my connection to the earth a degree or two less literal than it seemed on mushrooms?—but other philosophers have used drug experiences to support broader metaphysical claims than mine. Aldous Huxley (1894–1963) recounts his first experience with mescaline in his book *The Doors of Perception*. Huxley writes of being "shaken out of the ruts of ordinary perception, to be shown for a few timeless hours the outer and the inner world, not as they appear to an animal obsessed with survival or to a human being obsessed with words and notions, but as they are apprehended, directly and unconditionally, by Mind at Large."[9] Mescaline for Huxley offered a way of knowing things objectively, apart from his normal and limited perspective. "I was seeing what Adam had seen on the morning of his creation—the miracle, moment by moment, of naked existence."[10]

This is a pretty big claim, and we have to ask how it is that mescaline allows Huxley to see naked existence. Huxley's answer is that because mescaline precipitates ego loss, there is no sense of a seer who sees. Instead there is only what is seen in pure awareness, "Mind at Large." This raises a question: Is the state of there not *seeming* to be a seer the same as the state of there not being a seer? If not, then the feeling of pure awareness might be less real than *normal* awareness because even though the seer's perceptions are still influencing the seen, the awareness of that influence is lost. It is almost impossible to argue against the influence of subjectivity because we cannot get outside of our own subjectivity to have anywhere to argue from. Except, Huxley tells us, that when you experience pure awareness, you can tell your perceptions are *realer*. And for good reason.

Huxley appeals to the work of Dr. C. D. Broad (1887–1971), who describes the brain as a filter of the world's innumerable stimuli. Using Broad's theory, Huxley argues that mescaline and other hallucinogens turn off the reducing valves of our brains and give us short-term peeks into a less filtered, if not unfiltered, reality. Alice for her part never seems to experience true ego loss. Her perceptions and her sense of self are altered but never lost.[11] She sees differently but never with Huxley's "Mind at Large."

In *Cleansing the Doors of Perception*, Huston Smith (b. 1919) describes his first experience with entheogens. Like Huxley, Smith took mescaline (under the guidance of Timothy Leary, then of Harvard, at the suggestion of Huxley, who was a colleague of Smith's at MIT). Smith, a religious scholar, had studied mysticism and practiced meditation for decades "with disappointing results, I have to confess." He goes on: "I do not regret those years, and continue to meditate each day, but it does more to strengthen my life's trajectory and call me back to the here and now than it does to produce mystical visions and altered states of consciousness." As for those altered states of consciousness, Smith says, "when Huxley's *Doors of Perception* appeared, the mescaline it reported sounded like a Godsend—literally. . . . [Mescaline] introduced him to 'the flow of beauty to heightened beauty, from deeper to ever deeper meaning.' Perhaps it could do the same for me."[12]

Once Smith ingested the mescaline, "the layers of the mind, most of whose contents our conscious mind screens out to smelt the remainder down into a single band we can cope with, were now revealed in their completeness—spread out as if by spectroscope into about five distinguishable layers. . . . I was experiencing the metaphysical theory known as emanationism, in which, beginning with the clear, unbroken Light of the Void, that light then fractures into multiple forms and declines in intensity as it devolves through descending levels of reality."[13]

Just as my first psilocybin experience allowed me to experience directly my connection with nature, Smith's experience allowed him to see things he had previously understood only abstractly.

It's not important for our purposes what emanationism is all about. What is important is that (1) Smith saw things differently; and (2) what he saw felt overwhelmingly real. Something worth considering here is that Smith and I both saw what we were looking for. Most people who have used hallucinogenic drugs will know what I mean. Those who have not may get some sense of it from reading *Alice*. When Alice takes drugs they make her larger or smaller as she needs them to, but not always to the degree she'd like. This is the kind of control most people have of their drug experiences. There's room to guide, but not control. Timothy Leary talks about this in terms of "set": "The nature of the experience depends almost entirely on set and setting. Set denotes the preparation of the individual, including his personality structure and his mood at the time."[14] Drugs magnify what's already there.

Even before Huxley and Smith, the philosopher William James (1842–1910) experimented with drugs. Consider what he has to say about his experience with nitrous oxide:

> One conclusion was forced upon my mind at that time, and my impression of its truth has ever since remained unshaken. It is that our normal waking consciousness, rational consciousness as we call it, is but one special type of consciousness, whilst all about it, parted from it by the flimsiest of screens, there lie potential forms of consciousness entirely different. We may go through life without suspecting their existence; but apply the requisite stimulus, and at a touch they are there in all their completeness, definite types of mentality which probably somewhere have their field of application and adaptation. No account of the universe in its totality can be final which leaves these other forms of consciousness quite disregarded. How to regard them is the question—for they are so discontinuous with ordinary consciousness. Yet they may determine attitudes though they cannot furnish formulas, and open a region though they fail to give a map. At any rate, they forbid a premature closing of our accounts with reality. Looking back on my own experience, they all converge towards a kind of insight to which I cannot help ascribing some metaphysical significance. The keynote of it is invariably a reconciliation. It is as if the opposite of the world, whose contradictions and conflict make all our difficulties and troubles, were melted into unity.[15]

What's most valuable about this quote from James is the idea that we not discount experiences on drugs out of hand. They may or may not show us something more *real*, but they certainly show us something different.[16] And for that we must be able to take account when we speak of *reality*. The problems of dreams and trusting our own perceptions at any time (because of all the assumptions we naturally make) show us that we never have the authority to simply dismiss abnormal experiences, because by definition all of our experiences appear to us as our experiences. As Alan Watts points out: "[A] man who mistrusts himself cannot even trust his mistrust, and must therefore be hopelessly confused."[17]

The Real Is Fake and the Fake Is Real

Drugs and dreams dissolve the distinction between normal and distorted reality by calling to our attention the faulty assumptions under which this distinction is made. *Alice in Wonderland*—drug story, dream story, cultural myth—presents these dilemmas for us. In fact, it raises them so well that *Alice in Wonderland* (a drug trip inside a dream inside a fantasy inside two pieces of cardboard) has become the name for a real, diagnosable medical syndrome: it describes a condition where a person suffers from distorted space, time, and body image. Spells are temporary and often associated with migraines or psychoactive drugs. If that sends your mind spinning back and forth between fact and fiction, it should. The real is fake; the fake is real; and you must trust yourself to know what's what, keeping in mind of course that you must also trust your informed distrust. Drugs, dreams, and a little critical thinking go a long way toward showing us that our everyday waking life is a lot more like Alice's trip to Wonderland than we might normally think.

As for Alice, we know that when she wakes up she thinks to herself that she's had a wonderful dream. We assume such a wonderful dream will stick in her memory, but we don't expect it to feel real for her in the same way it felt real while she was dreaming it. In this respect, Alice's story differs from ours. When we wake from a dream, come down from a high, or return to normal reality from some other altered state, there is always the chance that the lingering traces of the experience will retain their credibility even as they lose their immediacy. If they don't retain their credibility, then we are, like Alice, occasionally mad, and *this*—normal reality—is all there really is. But if our distorted experiences do linger, as the mystical ones often seem to, maybe our normal experience of reality is partial. Whether distorted reality has anything to offer us is left to each of us to determine for ourselves. I follow William James in saying, "It must always remain an open question whether mystical states may not possibly be such superior points of view, windows through which the mind looks out upon a more extensive and inclusive world."[18] Most questions surrounding perception and reality are open ones. One of the only certainties is that the rabbit-hole is very deep indeed.

NOTES

1. Interestingly, Albert Hoffman invented LSD while searching for a cure for migraines, which Lewis Carroll suffered from, and some think influenced his writing about distorted reality.
2. One such allusion for those who are looking for such things might be Alice's inquiries into self-identity. Are the inquiries the rational response of a conscious being in the world—the human condition, sober or intoxicated—or are they meant to suggest the intense introspection often brought on by the drugs we associate with *Alice*, marijuana and hallucinogens?
3. I should reemphasize that I don't think *Alice's Adventures* are strictly drug stories the way *Fear and Loathing in Las Vegas* is; *Alice* is just well-suited to a drug reading in the way *The Matrix* is well-suited to a drug reading or a Christian reading or a Buddhist reading or a cyborg reading or many other readings.
4. Plato, *The Works of Plato* (New York: Random House, 1956), 502–503.
5. Lewis Carroll, *Alice's Adventures in Wonderland and Through the Looking-Glass* (New York: Penguin Putnam Inc., 2000), 65.
6. Ibid., 49.
7. Burton Watson, *Chuang Tzu: Basic Writings* (New York: Columbia University Press, 1996), 45.

8. Bertrand Russell, *The Problems of Philosophy* (Oxford: Oxford University Press, 1959), 8.

9. Aldous Huxley, *The Doors of Perception* (New York: Harper & Brothers, 1954), 73.

10. Ibid., 17.

11. I have in mind here the repeating theme of Alice's discontinuity of self.

12. Huston Smith, *Cleansing the Doors of Perception* (New York: Penguin Putnam, 2000), 6.

13. Ibid., 10–11.

14. Timothy Leary, Ralph Metzner, and Richard Alpert, *The Psychedelic Experience* (New York: Kensington, 1992), 11.

15. William James, *The Varieties of Religious Experience* (New York: Simon & Schuster, 1997), 305–306.

16. They may even help us to understand Hegel. NO_2 did for James. As he writes in his essay "Subjective Effects of Nitrous Oxide": "Some observations of the effects of nitrous-oxide-gas-intoxication . . . have made me understand better than ever before both the strength and the weakness of Hegel's philosophy."

17. Alan Watts, "Beat Zen, Square Zen, and Zen," *Chicago Review* 42 (1996): 50.

18. James, *The Varieties of Religious Experience*, 335.

PERSPECTIVISM AND TRAGEDY: A NIETZSCHEAN INTERPRETATION OF ALICE'S ADVENTURE

Rick Mayock

Alice has nothing to do, and she is bored. She's feeling sleepy—and the book her sister is reading has no pictures or conversations! But within a very short time, she finds herself burning with curiosity when a white rabbit with pink eyes hurries by, wearing a watch and a waistcoat, talking to itself about being late.

Actually, Alice doesn't think it very remarkable at all to see a talking rabbit with a watch and a waistcoat. When she thinks about it later, she wonders why something so extraordinary doesn't seem unusual to her. Perhaps she's more curious about the idea of a talking rabbit and the possibility of an exciting adventure than in an explanation of what is true or real.

The philosopher Friedrich Nietzsche (1844–1900) says we all do something like this—our "will to truth" conceals a "will to ignorance." In order to have knowledge or "truth," according to Nietzsche, we must first embrace some illusion and falsity.[1] We must, like artists, be the creators of our own meaning. Art, for Nietzsche, makes life meaningful, and tragedy, the highest form of art, makes life tolerable. We often find ourselves in situations where, like Alice, we are forced to construct a meaningful world in order to survive the chaos and the madness that surround us.

All of this, of course, needs some explanation. But let's take the Gryphon's advice: "Adventures first . . . explanations take such a dreadful time."[2]

"Important—Unimportant—Unimportant—Important"

According to Nietzsche, we are all a bit like Alice in our quest for knowledge. Alice's willingness to accept the appearance of the White Rabbit without question is an example of what Nietzsche calls the "will to ignorance."[3] Knowledge requires leaving some things out. So we must recognize the necessity of illusion in order to attain knowledge. Maybe this is what Alice is doing when she embraces her vision of the White Rabbit with a watch and waistcoat, muttering to itself as it hurries down the rabbit-hole.

Alice eagerly seeks out adventures as a way to make life more exciting. "Alice," we are told, "had got so much into the way of expecting nothing but out-of-the-way things to happen, that it seemed quite dull and stupid for life to go on in the common way."[4] Nietzsche also looks at the world as a succession of adventures that provide us with relief from the boredom of our lives. Our experiences are subject to many different interpretations or perspectives, and no one specific interpretation or perspective is the privileged or correct point of view. But in order to form one perspective we need to ignore many others. In this way we *create* "truth," though we convince ourselves that we have *discovered* it. Most philosophers, says Nietzsche, cannot distinguish between "finding" and "inventing." Like artists, we choose, select, and simplify our ideas about the world, but because of our will to ignorance, we believe we are not choosing, selecting, or simplifying. Like the King presiding over the trial, we sit in judgment of what counts as relevant to our lives: "Important—unimportant—unimportant—important,"[5] and we convince ourselves that our ideas give us a correct and accurate picture of the way things are.

Perhaps this is what Alice does when she chooses to overlook how odd the White Rabbit appears. Her desire for knowledge (or for an adventure) impels her to choose, to select, and to simplify what counts as real. This is how, according to Nietzsche, the will to ignorance is embedded in the will to truth. But this will to truth must always be viewed with suspicion. The will to truth is based on a retained ignorance that allows us to be like Alice and seek out life's adventures.[6]

Rabbit-Holes and Abysses

Alice chases the White Rabbit and tumbles down the rabbit-hole. As she descends, her perspectives begin to change significantly. Her normal ways of thinking about the world are challenged: her way of thinking about time, space, and distance. She wonders about people with their heads downward, and if cats eat bats, or if bats eat cats. The very foundations of what she considers to be true and real come into question as she tumbles down, down, down, and wonders if she will fall right through the earth.

It's comforting to think of the truth as something that is given, unshakable, and not subject to interpretations and fluctuations. We like to think of the truth as reliable and stable, as our ground or foundation. Philosophers often use this terminology when they refer to the "ground" of being, or when referring to someone or something as "grounded" in reality. But what if the ground were to suddenly fall away?

What if what we thought to be reality, what we took for granted, were to dissolve beneath our feet? Or what if our most cherished philosophical beliefs and assumptions about truth and reality turn out to be empty holes with no support or substance?

Nietzsche says we are always in danger of falling into abysses, for what we assume to be the ground, the stable, unchanging "reality," is merely a fiction. The belief in this ground is what he calls one of the prejudices of philosophers. Those who are aware of this lack of ground or presence of an unchanging "reality" he calls "free spirits," "a new species of philosopher."[7] They "dance near abysses" because they take nothing for granted and, like Alice, are conscious of the lack of ground beneath them. They construct a world in which their own values are manifested, and they have no pretence that their views represent objective reality. On her way down the rabbit-hole Alice begins to think like one of Nietzsche's free spirits. So many "out-of-the-way-things" are happening to Alice that she begins to think that very few things are really impossible.

Alice's adventure now becomes an exercise in controlling perspectives. Her experiences of growing, shrinking, and falling down the rabbit-hole change her perspective and move the narrative into situations that challenge her (and our) perceptions, which beg for newer interpretations and meanings. Like Alice, we create adventures to relieve us from a life of dullness and indifference. Sometimes we need to hear a good story, read a good book, or watch an interesting movie. Stories give us unique perspectives and help us to create meaning for our lives. When the stories end we are left with nothing but a meaningless void and we are back facing the abyss. In the Mouse's tale, the figure "Fury" also has "nothing to do," and threatens to prosecute the Mouse and condemn it to death. The Mouse's tale (tail) is a narrative that ends in the abyss of "death." As Alice's attention wanders, the Mouse is offended and wanders away. Like Alice, we too, depend on narratives that keep us engaged, keep our attention from wandering.

"I'm Not Myself, You See"

Alice's experimentation in perspectives takes a new turn when she encounters a large mushroom growing near her, about the same height as herself. She looks under it, on both sides of it, and behind it, and it occurs to her that she might as well look and see what's on top of it. Alice takes many different perspectives on the mushroom, but is there one point of view that is correct or most accurate? For Nietzsche, this question doesn't make sense, because there is no mushroom apart from our experience—only perspectives on the mushroom.

But, one might object, we can make a distinction between the appearances of the mushroom and the independently existing "reality" of the mushroom. There must be some absolute truth, some objective order in the world that is independent of and antecedent to our theories about the world. Nietzsche calls this desire for an independent reality another one of the prejudices of philosophers. Metaphysics, the branch of philosophy that pursues knowledge of this independent reality, is nothing more than a form of dogmatism. Philosophers who practice metaphysics are dogmatists because they present an interpretation of the world as the *only* legitimate interpretation. They claim that there is a true, fixed, privileged account of the universe, that facts exist independently of our knowing them and that reality is independent of our interpretations.

For Nietzsche there is no difference between the appearance of the mushroom and the mushroom itself. Reality is not something behind appearances; rather, we arrange our appearances into a perspective that enables us to survive and make sense of an otherwise formless flux, or what Nietzsche calls arrangements of "wills to power."[8] "Reality" is nothing more than the totality of these arrangements.

Alice stretches herself up on tiptoe to peek over the edge of the mushroom and discovers a large blue caterpillar sitting on top of it. The Caterpillar asks, "Who are you?," but Alice finds it difficult to give an adequate answer. She knows who she was when she got up that morning, but acknowledges that she has changed several times since then. When the Caterpillar demands an explanation, she can only say that she is not herself.

Alice is having a crisis of personal identity, and the Caterpillar's questions bring this crisis into focus. She can't identify who she is because of her changes in size and appearance, and the only way she can figure it out is by trying to remember who she was before she experienced all of the changes. But this doesn't work either: "It's no use going back to yesterday," Alice says to the Gryphon and the Mock Turtle, "because I was a different person then."[9]

According to Nietzsche, we all face a similar identity crisis. Nietzsche suggests that there is no real "self" or "ego" apart from our experiences. We are constantly changing and becoming new people, and there is no part of our selves that doesn't change. In effect, our concepts of "I" and "self" are static, unchanging mental constructs. But they are mere fictions and the result of the grammatical habit of linking an action to an agent who performs the action. The "doer," says Nietzsche, is merely a fiction added to the "deed."[10] So the "self" is a fiction that we create out of the assumption that there must be a doer for every deed. Just as there is no "lightning" behind the flash—only the flash itself—there is no "self" behind the activity of the "self," and no real distinction between "being" and "becoming." The error of the "self" is similar to the error of thinking there is a "mushroom" apart from our perspectives of the mushroom.

Alice tries to explain to the Caterpillar that it is emotionally difficult to go through such major changes. "When you have to turn into a chrysalis—you will some day, you know—and then after that into a butterfly, I should think you'll feel it a little queer, won't you?"[11] she asks the Caterpillar. But the Caterpillar doesn't think so, as if it knows that the "self" is just an illusion. The dramatic changes that we endure through life may be, Nietzsche suggests, the reason we cling to the illusion of an unchanging or enduring "self" that abides through the constant changes in appearances. Nietzsche claims that this is the motivation for belief in the fiction of the immortal "soul" that continues to exist after the body dies. But we must always be suspicious of such hidden motivations.

As Alice's size fluctuates, so do her perspectives, and these changes affect her cognition and memory. She can't accurately remember poems she has memorized, nor can she correctly do her multiplication tables. "So you think you're changed, do you?" asks the Caterpillar. She replies: "I can't remember things as I used—and I don't keep the same size for ten minutes together!"[12]

"Be What You Would Seem to Be"

With a little instruction from the Caterpillar, Alice learns to modulate her size (and her perspectives) by nibbling on different sides of the mushroom. Alice resembles one of Nietzsche's free spirits by taking control of her perspectives and by not pretending they are in any way an accurate account of the way things really are. Free spirits know that their mode of life is their own creation and that it is not the only possible mode. Unlike dogmatists, they do not impose their views on others. Free spirits pursue "truth" by adapting to their illusions while always retaining the awareness that they are illusions.[13]

Alice does exactly this when she adapts her size to visit the Duchess's house. She is immediately alarmed by what she finds there. The air is filled with pepper, the Cook is tossing plates and dishes at the Duchess, and the baby is howling. But in the midst of all this chaos, she manages to get the baby out of the house, where it begins to resemble a pig. "If it had grown up," she says to herself, "it would have made a dreadfully ugly child: but it makes a rather handsome pig, I think."[14] Finding the right perspective on things makes them more tolerable, and more aesthetically pleasing. From one perspective, a very ugly child is in the making, from another perspective, a handsome pig.

Alice speculates about other children who would be better off as pigs, "if one only knew the right way to change them."[15] The more we can control our perspectives, the more the world makes sense to us. When Alice sees the Cheshire Cat in a tree, she asks it for advice: "Would you tell me, please, which way I ought to go from here?" "That depends a good deal on where you want to get to," says the Cat.[16] The Cheshire Cat's response acknowledges that we are the creative artists of our lives when we select our own perspectives. As the Duchess says to Alice: "Be what you would seem to be."[17]

The Cheshire Cat has a curious way of fading in and out of existence. When enough of its mouth appears, it speaks. Alice waits until its eyes appear before she nods, and waits until its ears appear, or at least one of them, before speaking to it. The Cheshire Cat typifies the transitory and ephemeral nature of truth as Nietzsche sees it. To use Nietzsche's formulation, there is no "cat" existing apart from the appearances of the cat, or, more precisely, apart from Alice's experiences of the cat. To assume the "cat" exists as a substance independent of our perspectives is another one of the errors or prejudices of philosophers. As perspectives fade, the Cheshire Cat fades, illustrating the transitory nature of "truth."

"No Wise Fish Would Go Anywhere without a Porpoise"

When Alice becomes more skilled at changing her size by nibbling on the mushroom, she finds her way into a beautiful garden, and walks among the bright flower beds. There she immediately encounters more chaos and confusion, beginning with gardeners who are painting the white roses red. She learns that the gardeners are falsifying the color of the roses in order to please the Queen. Nietzsche suggests that we, too, "falsify" our cognitive vision of the world to suit our purposes and thereby create the illusion of artistic completeness. Just as a painter can never paint "everything" and attain representational completeness, we, too, in our understanding, arrange, select, and simplify our knowledge of the world.

The garden becomes the setting for a kind of tragedy in which Alice is the victim of the arbitrary whims of the other characters, especially, the Queen, who shows up threatening to behead the gardeners. The Queen then invites Alice to play a game of croquet. Alice consents, but quickly becomes frustrated with the lack of order to the game. She complains to the Cheshire Cat: "They don't seem to have any rules in particular, at least, if there are, nobody attends to them—and you've no idea how confusing it is all the things being alive."[18] The flamingos will not remain croquet mallets, and the hedgehogs will not stay rolled up but continually run away.

Alice is catapulted into a world with no rules, which induces her (and us) to try to make sense out of the nonsense. The caucus race is chaotic: "The best way to explain it is to do it,"[19] says the Dodo. The exact shape of the racecourse doesn't matter. The participants begin running when they like and leave off when they like, and everybody wins a prize. Of course it's always teatime for the Hatter, the March Hare, and the Dormouse. And the trial proceeds in a confused way, with no clear verdict.

For Nietzsche, there is no order to nature, and the impulse to impose any rational order must be eyed with suspicion. The need for order is a human requirement, something that we impose on the chaotic flux that is merely an arrangement of arbitrary wills to power. This idea is illustrated by the Hatter's riddle: "Why is a raven like a writing-desk?" A raven, a predatory and instinctual representative of nature, operates by no rules or regulations, but a writing desk represents civilization and imposed order. The riddle may have no satisfactory answer, as Alice tells the Hatter: "I think you might do something better with the time than wasting it in asking riddles that have no answers."[20] Riddles with no clear answers remind us that our knowledge is incomplete, but they also force us to think about familiar things in new and unusual ways.

Alice longs for some familiar signposts of an intelligible order amidst the chaos. She attempts to invent some rules that will make sense of the nonsensical world in which she finds herself. When she sees the Duchess in a pleasant temper she thinks to herself, "Maybe it's always the pepper that makes people hot-tempered."[21] She is very much pleased at having found a new kind of rule. It's reassuring to discover a rule that works and that helps us to navigate through chaotic seas. But how easy it is to misappropriate rules and maxims in situations to which they may not apply. The Duchess does this with her compulsive moralizing: "How fond she is of finding morals in things!"[22] Alice says to herself.

More chaos and nonsense confront Alice during the trial, which quickly becomes a meaningless and arbitrary administration of justice. "If there's no meaning in it," says the King about a spurious letter introduced as evidence, "that saves a world of trouble, you know, as we needn't try to find any."[23] Nietzsche would agree with the King—there is no meaning to find. But the "world of trouble" comes when we attempt to create meaning when there is no "meaning" to find, and solve riddles that can't be solved. We impose form on the formless, which allows us to make decisions about how to proceed in life. In other words, we try to see our lives within a larger purpose.

As the Mock Turtle suggests: "No wise fish would go anywhere without a porpoise."[24]

Dull Reality: The Tragic View of Life

Alice can be seen as a tragic heroine in her attempt to remain poised and act heroically as the Queen threatens to behead everyone.[25] To survive, she must establish some sense of order within a morally unintelligible void. She attempts to do this by imposing her will on the disorder and by contriving rules to aid her navigation through the mindless chaos, madness, and anarchy that threaten her sanity and her safety.

According to Nietzsche, nature requires the supplement of art for its own creatures to exist in a meaningful way.[26] Art, for Nietzsche, reaches its highest expression in Greek tragedy. Nietzsche suggests that tragedy provides us with the insight that the ultimate nature of the world is such that it has no orderly structure. Tragedy also reminds us that it is we who impose order and purpose on an otherwise chaotic and formless world.

According to Nietzsche's analysis, tragedy is created under two powerful influences: the Apollonian and the Dionysian.[27] The Greek god Apollo brings the influence of order, form, clarity, individuality, restraint, and rationality to the aesthetic experience. The Apollonian vision stands as a dream in comparison to ordinary waking life. It gives delight in the beauty of images, and extends a state of calm repose to the individual. Alice exemplifies this when she remains, for the most part, in an Apollonian dream state, calm and reposed, despite falling down the rabbit-hole—an otherwise terrifying experience. The god Dionysus inspires instinctual behavior, intense emotion, sensuality, intoxication, frenzy, and madness. The Hatter and the March Hare best exemplify this attitude, since they are both mad. Under the influence of Dionysian intoxication, the individual loses the certainty of a separate "self" and merges into the larger whole in an ecstatic celebration.

Although tragedy reveals to us that the world lacks order and rules, it offers consolation by showing us that we are no different from the rest of nature, as Alice realizes she is just one among many characters in the story. On the one hand, tragedy reminds us that we are, under the influence of Apollo, separate individuals. On the other hand, the Dionysian influence allows us to merge and become one with the world. Tragedy thus provides us with some comfort: what Nietzsche calls a "metaphysical joy," which enables the audience to feel that they, too, belong to the deeper reality behind all phenomena.[28]

The story of Alice provides us with metaphysical respite from the chaos, disquietude, and indifference of reality. Alice's curiosity and her experimentation with perspectivism induce the reader to develop an interestedness, much in the way that tragedy invites our interestedness in life and helps make it tolerable for us. Alice expresses mixed emotion as she muses on her fate: "I almost wish I hadn't gone down the rabbit-hole— and yet—and yet—it's rather curious, you know, this sort of life! I do wonder what can have happened to me! When I used to read fairy tales I fancied that kind of thing never happened, and now here I am in the middle of one!"[29]

When Alice awakens from her adventure, she tells her sister about the characters and creatures she has encountered in Wonderland. Alice's sister longs for a similar experience, and muses about how these strange tales relieve us from the boredom and dullness of our everyday existence. They brighten the ordinary with excitement and allow us to transcend the commonplace, at least for a while. Alice's sister sits with her eyes closed, half believing herself in Wonderland, but knows that when she opens them again, all will change back to "dull reality."

Tragedy provides the metaphysical comfort that life is, as Nietzsche suggests, "despite all the changes of appearance, indestructibly powerful and pleasurable."[30] Under the influence of Dionysus, tragedy teaches us that life is to be celebrated. As Alice goes off to enjoy the rest of her summer, we are left with intoxicating memories of Wonderland and the celebration of youth. We are also left wondering about exactly what the Cheshire Cat means when it says: "We're all mad here."[31]

NOTES

1. Nietzsche develops this idea in *Beyond Good and Evil*, trans. Walter Kaufman (New York: Vintage Books, 1966). "The will to knowledge," he writes, is based on a hidden motive, "on the foundation of a far more powerful will: the will to ignorance, to the uncertain, to the untrue!" (35).
2. Lewis Carroll, *Alice's Adventures in Wonderland* (London: Penguin Books, 1998), 91.
3. Nietzsche, *Beyond Good and Evil*, 35.
4. Carroll, *Alice's Adventures*, 15.
5. Ibid., 103.
6. Nietzsche writes, "From the beginning we have contrived to retain our ignorance in order to enjoy an almost inconceivable freedom, lack of scruple and caution, heartiness and gaiety of life—in order to enjoy life!" (*Beyond Good and Evil*, 35).
7. Ibid., 10–11.
8. Ibid., 21.
9. Carroll, *Alice's Adventures*, 91.
10. Friedrich Nietzsche, *On the Genealogy of Morals*, trans. Walter Kaufmann and R. J. Hollingdale (New York: Vintage Books, 1967), 45.
11. Carroll, *Alice's Adventures*, 41.
12. Ibid., 42.
13. "To recognize untruth as a condition of life," Nietzsche writes, "that certainly means resisting accustomed value feelings in a dangerous way; and a philosophy that risks this would by that token alone place itself beyond good and evil" (*Beyond Good and Evil*, 12).
14. Carroll, *Alice's Adventures*, 55–56.
15. Ibid., 56.

16. Ibid.
17. Ibid., 80.
18. Ibid., 75.
19. Ibid., 26.
20. Ibid., 62–63.
21. Ibid., 78.
22. Ibid., 79.
23. Ibid., 106.
24. Ibid., 90.
25. Donald Rackin makes this point in "Blessed Rage: Lewis Carroll and the Modern Quest for Order," in *Alice in Wonderland: A Norton Critical Edition*, 2nd edition, ed. Donald J. Gray (New York: W.W. Norton and Co. 1992). "She [Alice] thus becomes for many modern readers what she undoubtably was for Dodgson: a naïve champion of the doomed human quest for ultimate meaning and Edenic order." Alice can be viewed as a tragic heroine, but ultimately, Rackin writes, "has the practical good sense of a comic, rather than a tragic, heroine" (ibid., 402).
26. This is a common theme in Nietzsche's writings. "The existence of the world is justified only as an aesthetic phenomenon" (*The Birth of Tragedy*, trans. Walter Kaufmann [New York: Vintage Books, 1967], 22). Or again, "We possess art lest we perish of the truth" (*The Will to Power*, trans. Walter Kaufmann and R. J. Hollingdale [New York: Vintage Books, 1967], 435).
27. Nietzsche develops these themes in *The Birth of Tragedy*, 33–93.
28. Nietzsche writes, "This is the most immediate effect of the Dionysian tragedy, that the state and society, and, quite generally, the gulfs between man and man give way to an overwhelming feeling of unity leading back to the very heart of nature" (ibid., 59).
29. Carroll, *Alice's Adventures*, 32–33.
30. Nietzsche, *The Birth of* Tragedy, 59.
31. Carroll, *Alice's Adventures*, 57.

WISHING IT WERE SOME OTHER TIME: THE TEMPORAL PASSAGE OF ALICE

Mark W. Westmoreland

The philosopher St. Augustine (354–430) once mused, "What is this time? If no one asks me, I know; if I want to explain it to a questioner, I do not know."[1] Alice probably feels the same way. The master of nonsense, Lewis Carroll, brilliantly calls time into question by challenging the way in which Alice, and each one of us, understands the nature of time. Is time a substance? Is it something external to us, akin, perhaps, to planetary motion? Or is time, rather, something we impose on the world in order to make sense of our own experiences? Perhaps the Hatter, who speaks of time as a personal acquaintance, isn't so mad after all when he stresses the qualitative, experiential dimension of time.

Augustine: Always Changing, Always Now

In Book XI of his *Confessions*, Augustine raises the question of time in relation to creation, concluding that there was no time prior to the creation of the world. Consequently, it would be foolish to ask what God was doing *before* creation. For God, there was no before because the term "before" applies to temporal things. God exists in an "ever-present eternity."[2] According to Augustine, God created time at the exact moment that God created the physical world. There simply was no time before the world was created.

Augustine then raises the more difficult question of what time actually is: "If nothing passed there would be no past time; if nothing were approaching, there would be no future time; if nothing were, there would be no present time."[3] How, then, can we conceive of the past and future as real if neither exists in the present? The past is no longer now and the future has not yet come to be. Alice intuitively discovers this about herself. While speaking with the Caterpillar, she says, "I—I hardly know, Sir, just at the present—at least I know who I *was* when I got up this morning, but I think I must have been changed several times since then."[4] Indeed, Alice is continually changing. Even the present fades into the past and is directed toward nonexistence. For example, when a person says "Lewis Carroll," there is a different now when pronouncing "-oll" than when pronouncing "Lew-." While Alice is confused about how she is changing, the Caterpillar, who already knows that life—his own life from a caterpillar to a butterfly—is all about change, tells her that she will "get used to it in time."[5] Sooner or later, Alice, like all people, will discover that her life is filled with transformation. With all this change, Alice can only experience the immediate present. So how can we speak of past and future if the present is all that exists?

Augustine reconciles the existence of past, present, and future by placing all three times within the present. Each time exists only in the present as "a present of things past, a present of things present, [and] a present of things future."[6] On the one hand, we attempt to measure the *length* of time. On the other, we cannot measure that which no longer exists (the past) or that which is not yet (the future). Augustine resolves this in two stages. First, time is not the movement of objects over an extended space. Therefore time cannot be measured empirically, by the senses and experimentation. Second, time is a mental construct experienced in the present. Thus the measurement of time is the measurement of impressions of things passing through the mind in the present. When Alice encounters the Mock Turtle and the Gryphon, she is better aware that her existence is marked by change: "I could tell you my adventures—beginning from this morning, but it's no use going back to yesterday, because I was a different person then."[7] She knows that the past no longer exists in itself; rather, the past exists only as her memories in the present. Even though Alice can no longer experience past events, she can recall them to her mind in the now. Following this illustration, we can think of the past as the experience of memory in the present, and the future as the present expectation of a time to come.

Kant: It's All in Your Head

Like Augustine, the philosopher Immanuel Kant (1724–1804) places temporality within human consciousness. In the *Critique of Pure Reason*, Kant claims that time is the necessary condition for the possibility of experience. In other words, time is an intuition of the mind that Alice must have in order for her to have any sort of adventure. For Kant, time is already presupposed in an experience, in order to allow for a person to grasp relations such as "at the same time" or "succeeding in time." *Alice's Adventures in Wonderland* begins with Alice watching the White Rabbit getting anxious about being late: "Oh dear! Oh dear! I shall be too late!"[8] The White Rabbit has not yet experienced the actual future event. What he experiences now is the expectation of a time to come. He understands that the present is prior to the future event; hence, he is presently anxious.

Kant draws the three conclusions: (1) Time is not something that exists by itself. (2) Time is actually a psychological sense by which we engage the world. (3) As this sense or
intuition, time is prior to any particular engagement that one
may have with the world.[9] Kant's conclusions reveal an interpretation of temporality that describes time as a subjective and
formal condition for human experience. Time is in our minds.
Our perception of two sequential events testifies to this. Before
event A and the following event B ever occur, we already have
the intuition of time. Therefore, once event A occurs and then
event B occurs afterward, we understand that B followed A
and not vice versa. Without this intuition, we might think that
the year 2001 came before 1999, or that this morning came
before last night. Fortunately, we know better than this. Just as
Alice exclaims before the Red and White Queens in *Through
the Looking-Glass*, we can be sure that "there's only one day at
a time."[10]

Bergson I: Running to Stay Still

Time is commonly thought to be a movement of objects
from one point to another. The philosopher Henri Bergson
(1859–1941) challenged this conception of time in a way that
makes sense for Lewis Carroll. Zeno of Elea (fifth century BCE)
tells the story of a race between Achilles and a tortoise, in which
the tortoise is given a head start. According to Zeno, this creates a paradox. Achilles will never catch the tortoise and will
in fact lose the race. For each runs the race step by step, and
the tortoise, who has the head start, should always be one step
ahead. Lewis Carroll takes up the story in "What the Tortoise
Said to Achilles," depicting a conversation between the two at
the end of the race:

> Achilles had overtaken the Tortoise, and had seated
> himself comfortably on its back.

"So you've got to the end of our race-course?" said the Tortoise. "Even though it does consist of an infinite series of distances? I thought some wiseacre [Zeno] or other had proved that the thing couldn't be done?"

"It *can* be done," said Achilles. "It *has* been done! *Solvitur ambulando.* You see the distances were constantly *diminishing*; and so—"

"But if they had been constantly *increasing*?" the Tortoise interrupted. "How then?"

"Then I shouldn't be *here*," Achilles modestly replied; "and you would have got several times round the world, by this time!"[11]

While Zeno may have been confused about the nature of space, we're all confused about the nature of time, partly because we tend to think of time in terms of space. When we measure time we think of it in terms of space. But for Bergson time cannot be reduced to space; "as soon as we try to measure it, we unwittingly replace it by space."[12] To think spatially is not to think properly about time. Bergson explains that time is "duration," and duration is real regardless of whether space has been traversed or not. In the second chapter of *Through the Looking-Glass*, "The Garden of Live Flowers," Alice and the Red Queen illustrate this quite well:

"Now! Now!" cried the Queen. "Faster! Faster!" And they went so fast that at last they seemed to skim through the air, hardly touching the ground with their feet . . .

The Queen propped her up against a tree and said kindly, "You may rest a little now."

Alice looked round her in great surprise. "Why, I do believe we've been under this tree the whole time! Everything's just as it was!"

"Of course it is," said the Queen.[13]

Alice expected to be in a different location because the act of running occurred in duration. Through the Queen's explanation, however, Alice comes to recognize that they have experienced duration and change even though they have not actually moved across space. Everything changes regardless of spatiality.

Because each present is uniquely different from all others, the human perceiver does not have access to the present as such. Rather, a person has access to the quality of that which is experienced. The quality of time varies depending on a person's mental state. Moods condition everyday experiences. For example, a guy who is happy to be with his girlfriend will find that "time flies" when the two are together. A bored student will feel as if an average lecture "lasted for hours." No doubt, people are aware that some experiences feel longer or shorter than others; yet, when questioned, they will appeal to the mathematical time of discrete, homogenous instants. They will return to the idea that every moment is quantitatively equal in terms of seconds, minutes, hours, and so on. This, in turn, fails to account for the qualitative nature of experience that leads a person to describe his or her experience by using expressions such as "time flies." Not every moment feels the same. Sometimes an hour passes too quickly, and sometimes an hour lasts forever.

Bergson often contrasts his notion of duration with the paradoxes of Zeno, in which time is reduced to the movement of an entity from one position to another.[14] Motion contains the following two elements: (1) the homogenous, divisible space that is traversed, and (2) the indivisible, consciously real act of traversing. Zeno's mistake, according to Bergson, "arises from [his] identification of this series of acts, each of which is of a definite kind and indivisible, with the homogenous space which underlies them."[15] Bergson notes that we divide space into units such as meters, centimeters, millimeters, and so on; or, as in the world beyond the looking glass, the world is "marked out just like a large chess-board!"[16] While space is infinitely divisible as extension, it would be a mistake to equate two simultaneous positions in space with the movement of objects across space. Although each square on a chessboard is equal in size, Alice's experiences of the Fourth Square—that of Tweedledum and Tweedledee—and the Sixth Square—that of Humpty Dumpty— are uniquely and qualitatively different. And, of course, even if an object appears to remain in place, it is ceaselessly changing. You have changed since you started reading this chapter; you are older. Imagine the following: A person stares at a sheet of paper for three minutes. Did the paper change? The person responds in the negative. However, this person accepts the idea that the paper will deteriorate over centuries. This would be true even if the paper were to remain in the same position for many centuries. We can conclude that the negative response given initially was based on confusing duration and change with space. We are simply used to change occurring over a period of time.

Change is indivisible despite the common way of understanding temporality as mathematical clock time. Recognizing some truth to this, Alice becomes "dreadfully puzzled."

> Alice had been looking over his shoulder with some curiosity. "What a funny watch!" she remarked. "It tells the day of the month, and doesn't tell what o'clock it is!"
>
> "Why should it?" muttered the Hatter. "Does *your* watch tell you what year it is?"
>
> "Of course not," Alice replied very readily: "but that's because it stays the same year for such a long time together."
>
> "Which is just the case with *mine*," said the Hatter.[17]

The point is that we impose the second, minute, and hour on time. These things are not time itself. Our method of quantifying time is somewhat arbitrary. Would a year be experienced differently depending on how Alice quantitatively measures it? Perhaps not. Bergson writes, "When I follow with my eyes on the dial of a clock the movement of the hand which corresponds to the oscillations of the pendulum, I do not measure duration, as seems to be thought; I merely count simultaneities, which is very different."[18] Pure duration cannot be measured, however. Once Alice is through the looking glass, she sees that the back of the clock has "got the face of a little old man" and is grinning at her.[19] Why does he grin? Because he knows that the common way time is understood in Alice's world is not applicable beyond the looking glass. Nor is the common way really an accurate description of time for our world. Duration is continuous, indivisible time; it cannot be reduced to mathematical quantification and broken up into equivalent units such as minutes. We cannot divide an hour into sixty quantitative minutes and remain authentic to the various qualitative experiences within the hour, since not every minute is experienced in the same way.

Quantitative time is divided into spatialized units. When we attempt to measure time, we break it up into discontinuous points or seconds. Then, we must ask, what is between any two seconds? Smaller units of time. What are between these smaller units? Even smaller units of time. And this can go on forever. To think of time as seconds is to think of a long line of immobile points, but you will never be able to account for what propels time from one point to another by staring at a clock. You cannot know that one instant is different from another because this would require that you perceive two instants at once, which is not possible.

Portraying reality as immobile was the cause of Zeno's paradoxes. Zeno confused indivisible motion with the space traversed. Bergson claims that if we were to ask him, Achilles would make a remarkable statement:

> Zeno insists that I [Achilles] go from the point where I am to the point the tortoise has left, from that point to the next point it has left, etc., etc., that is his procedure

for making me run. But I go about it otherwise. I take a first step, then a second, and so on: finally, after a certain number of steps, I take a last one by which I skip ahead of the tortoise. I thus accomplish a series of indivisible acts.[20]

The race between Achilles and the tortoise cannot be divided like the space through which the race occurred. There is no immobility in reality in so far as real existence implies change. Likewise, "If movement is not everything it is nothing."[21] In other words, all is undergoing ceaseless change.

Bergson II: Teatime

Prior to the invention of clocks, most people understood time in relation to their daily activities, for example, farming. As the seasons change, the amount of sunlight varies and, consequently, the length of a day changes: "Twenty-four hours, I *think*; or is it twelve?"[22] A person might work in the field for fifteen hours daily during the summer but only ten during the winter. As we began using clocks, temporality, as we understood it, changed from heterogeneous and qualitative to homogenous and quantitative. According to Bergson, all existence implies change and duration that are real regardless of human perception. Even if no objects are actively traversing space, they are ceaselessly changing.

> "Well, I'd hardly finished the first verse," said the Hatter, "when the Queen bawled out, 'He's murdering time! Off with his head!'"
>
> "How dreadfully savage!" exclaimed Alice.
>
> "And ever since that," the Hatter went on in a mournful tone, "he won't do a thing I ask! It's always six o'clock now."
>
> A bright idea came into Alice's head. "Is that the reason so many tea things are put out here?" she asked.

"Yes, that's it," said the Hatter with a sigh: "it's always teatime, and we've no time to wash the things between whiles."

"Then you keep moving round, I suppose?" said Alice.

"Exactly so," said the Hatter: "as things get used up."[23]

Has time actually ceased for the Hare and Hatter, since it is always six o'clock? Of course not. They have returned to a world in which time is understood according to activities such as teatime.

Thinking of time in terms of a clock considers the present in mathematical terms as an instant analogous to a point on a line. But Bergson says this is an abstraction with no real existence. "You could never create time out of such instants any more than you could make a line out of mathematical points."[24] In between two points, say A and B, are an infinite number of other points. Clock time cannot account for the relation between the points and the catalyst by which the immobile becomes mobile. Again, this is due to the confusion of time with space.

What can we say about the present? Bergson's concept of the present is a significant modification of the Augustinian present. The present is usually thought to exist, whereas the past no longer exists and the future has not yet come into existence. For Augustine, the past and future survive in the present. Bergson asserts that the past preserves itself automatically by affecting the present. Without her falling down the rabbit-hole, Alice would not meet the Hatter. Once she meets the Hatter, her falling does not disappear; rather, it gets incorporated into the present. The present, for Bergson, varies by how a person pays attention to his or her experience. We are continually being inscribed upon by our past. "Our present," for Bergson, "falls back into the past when we cease to attribute to it an immediate interest."[25] In a sense, the present is only apparent to us whenever we focus on it. It is not a single instant; rather, it is our perceived experience. "My present," writes Bergson, "is the sentence I am pronouncing. But it is so because I want to limit the field of my attention to my sentence. This attention is something that can be made longer or shorter."[26] Think about a melody played on a piano. Imagine that you listen to the entire piece. That is your experience. If you were to break it up into sections it would be experienced quite differently—as multiple melodies.

Recall the Cheshire Cat's good-bye to Alice:

> "You'll see me there," said the Cat, and vanished.
>
> Alice was not much surprised at this, she was getting so well used to queer things happening. While she was still looking at the place where it had been, it suddenly appeared again.
>
> "Bye-the-bye, what became of the baby?" said the Cat. "I'd nearly forgotten to ask."
>
> "It turned into a pig." Alice quietly said, just as if it had come back in a natural way.
>
> "I thought it would," said the Cat, and vanished again. . . .
>
> "I said 'pig'," replied Alice; "and I wish you wouldn't keep appearing and vanishing so suddenly: you make one quite giddy!"[27]

At what point in time could we possibly say that the Cat was no longer present? We see here that the Cat slowly fades away, as if into the past. Sooner or later, the Cat would have no longer been before Alice. (Cats do not live forever, and neither will Alice.) It just happened more quickly than expected on this occasion.

What can be said of the nature of the future is far more difficult. It seems that we can describe it as open and free. Like Alice, you never know what will happen next. What we can know for certain is that we will never be the same.

Deleuze: Jam Today

To conclude, let's turn to Gilles Deleuze's portrayal of temporality in *The Logic of Sense*. Deleuze (1925–1995), who was significantly influenced by Bergson, claims that there are two readings of time: *chronos* and *aion*. According to chronos, "past, present, and future are not three dimensions of time; only the present fills time, whereas past and future are two dimensions relative to the present in time."[28] The present absorbs these two dimensions into itself. Past and future are excesses within the lived present. Thinking in terms of clock time, these excesses are regulated by the present and are, therefore, subject to measurement. This measurement is only possible by thinking that things are static and not changing. If we take things to be static and measurable according to equivalent units, then we arrive at clock time.

According to aion, there is no present as such. It is time of the event, of experience. Only the past and future exist.

> "It's very good jam," said the Queen.
>
> "Well, I don't want any *to-day*, at any rate."
>
> "You couldn't have it if you *did* want it," the Queen said. "The rule is, jam to-morrow and jam yesterday—but never jam to-day."
>
> "It *must* come sometimes to 'jam to-day'," Alice objected.
>
> "No it can't," said the Queen. "It's jam every *other* day: to-day isn't any other day, you know."[29]

According to the Queen, we will never have our jam. For Deleuze, today never comes. It is always yesterday and tomorrow together. That which we call "present" is the dynamic rupture of temporality. Rather than absorbing the past and future into itself, the present is divided by an infinitely expanding past and future in both directions at once. It would be even more correct to say that the present does not exist. A ceaseless rupture occurs in the meeting of the past and future in which these two are continually crashing against one another according to various intensities that allow for the qualitative nature of duration. "Aion," according to Deleuze, "is the past-future, which in an infinite subdivision of the abstract moment endlessly decomposes itself in both directions at once and forever sidesteps the present."[30] Consequently, we do not have access to a present as such since the abstract moment of the present is a "coming and going." It is always already gone and always coming but never now.

Our existence, like Alice's, is marked by ceaseless change, by an ever-growing radical altering of the self. After her adventures are over, Alice will never be the same. But are our adventures ever truly over? I certainly hope not. "I'd rather finish my tea" than stop living in the adventurous wonderland we call life.[31]

NOTES

1. Augustine, *Confessions*, trans. F. J. Sneed (Indianapolis: Hackett Publishing Company, Inc., 1993), XI. xiv, 219.
2. Augustine, *Confessions*, XI. xiii, 218.
3. Ibid., XI. xiv, 219.
4. Lewis Carroll, *Alice's Adventures in Wonderland and Through the Looking-Glass* (New York: Barnes and Noble Classics, 2004), 55. Subsequent references to the *Alice* stories are to this text.
5. Carroll, *Alice's Adventures*, 61.
6. Augustine, *Confessions*, XI. xx, 223.
7. Carroll, *Alice's Adventures*, 119.
8. Ibid., 13.
9. Immanuel Kant, *Critique of Pure Reason*, trans. J. M. D. Meiklejohn (Amherst, NY: Prometheus Books, 1990), 30.
10. Carroll, *Through the Looking-Glass*, 257.
11. Carroll, "What the Tortoise Said to Achilles," in *Alice's Adventures in Wonderland and Through the Looking-Glass*, 270.
12. Henri Bergson, *Time and Free Will*, trans. F. L. Pogson (Mineola, NY: Dover Publications, Inc., 2001), 106.
13. Carroll, *Through the Looking-Glass*, 175.

14. See Bergson's "The Perception of Change" in *The Creative Mind*, trans. Mabelle L. Andison (New York: Citadel Press, 2002).
15. Bergson, *Time and Free Will*, 113.
16. Carroll, *Through the Looking-Glass*, 173.
17. Carroll, *Alice's Adventures*, 81.
18. Bergson, *Time and Free Will*, 108.
19. Carroll, *Through the Looking-Glass*, 159.
20. Bergson, "The Perception of Change," 145.
21. Ibid.
22. Carroll, *Alice's Adventures*, 71.
23. Ibid., 83.
24. Bergson, "The Perception of Change," 151.
25. Ibid., 152.
26. Ibid., 151.
27. Carroll, *Alice's Adventures*, 75–76.
28. Gilles Deleuze, *The Logic of Sense*, trans. Mark Lester (New York: Columbia University Press, 1990), 162.
29. Carroll, *Through the Looking-Glass*, 205.
30. Deleuze, *The Logic of Sense*, 77.
31. Carroll, *Alice's Adventures*, 131.

PART FOUR

"WHO IN THE WORLD AM I?"

SERIOUS NONSENSE

Charles Taliaferro and Elizabeth Olson

Lewis Carroll's work has been interpreted in the most astonishing ways: as an encoded, esoteric philosophy of mystical love (according to Sherry Ackerman in her fascinating book, *Behind the Looking Glass*[1]), a meditation on and recovery of childhood (as suggested by W. H. Auden[2]), a work about the mastering of boredom and desire (Tan Lin[3]), and so on. In any case, Carroll's work is certainly appreciated as a treasure of philosophical puzzles. Perhaps because of this esteem, G. K. Chesterton hit the mark when he wrote that "Carroll's words should be read by sages and gray-haired philosophers . . . in order to study the darkest problems of metaphysics, the borderland between reason and unreason, and the nature of the most erratic of spiritual forces, humor, which eternally dances between the two."[4]

Following Chesterton's suggestion, this chapter investigates Carroll's use of humorous nonsense on the borderland between reason and unreason. In particular, we examine how far nonsense can be stretched before it is no longer humorous or insightful. Ridicule, satire, absurdity, and nonsense have a regular role in popular culture in stand-up routines, *The Daily*

Show, *Black Adder*, the classic *Monty Python's Flying Circus* and its spinoff movies like *Monty Python's The Meaning of Life*, and so on. But how far can one go in terms of absurdity or nonsense? You can make nonsense out of presidential candidates on *Saturday Night Live*, and you can even make fun of yourself when making fun of someone else (*SNL* can do a skit about *SNL*). But there is a sense in which not everything can be nonsense or absurd, and this is borne out by Lewis Carroll's work and also by a philosophical tradition that accords with Carroll's work. The word "absurdity" comes from the Latin term *absurdus*, meaning out of *tune*. You can only be out of tune if there is a tune or some idea of a tune that you are out of.

Let's begin with some philosophical background: the use of nonsense in ancient Greek philosophy to help set the stage for considering Carroll's contribution.

Nonsense in Ancient Greek Philosophy

Some of the early dialogues of Plato (427–347 BCE) feature Socrates (469–399 BCE) confronting his fellow Athenians who believe that they possess knowledge. Euthyphro, for example, claims to know what holiness or piety is, and that he is acting from this knowledge to bring a legal case against his father. Socrates questions Euthyphro, only to discover through a process of questions and replies, arguments and counterarguments, that Euthyphro does not actually know what he is talking about. In a word, Euthyphro's understanding of holiness or piety turns out to be *nonsense*. Other Platonic dialogues feature Socrates challenging those who claim to know about the nature of courage, friendship, love, justice, and so on. Socrates' strategy might be seen as a rude kind of ridicule blended with heaps of irony (in which he initially compliments his interlocutor only to later go in for the argumentative kill), but it may also be seen as a caring, humble device by which human pride is exposed as absurd or resting on nonsensical assumptions.

(Evidence of Socrates' caring and even love for his conversation partners might seem hyperbolic, but in the dialogue *Euthyphro*, Socrates reports that he must follow the arguments of Euthyphro the way a lover follows the beloved.)[5]

In an example that reminds us of Lewis Carroll, Plato uses nonsense as a humbling and humorous device in the *Republic*, Book 9. The question is raised about how much more pleasant a good king's life is than the tyrant's; the answer: seven hundred and twenty-nine times.[6] Although Socrates argues mathematically for this answer, arriving at such a number (we believe) is intended as nonsense—not unlike some of Carroll's playful puzzles—and to humorously rebuke, in this case, those who might decide which life to live based on a mathematics of pleasure.

More dramatically, one of the early Greco-Roman moral philosophers, Diogenes of Sinope (404–323 BCE), built his reputation largely upon exposing what he thought was the nonsense of tyranny. Diogenes was one of the few ancient philosophers who actually believed that slavery was wrong (this was definitely the exception, given the almost-universal practice of slavery in the ancient world). In one story of his life, Diogenes is captured and put up for sale. When asked what he would be good for, he replied, "Govern men!" He then "told the crier [announcer] to give notice in case anybody wanted to purchase a master for himself."[7] In this incident, Diogenes holds up the practice of slavery as nonsense.

Note that for Plato and Diogenes not everything was nonsense or absurd. For both philosophers the nonsense is funny, insightful, or philosophical because it is built on a conception of something good: a protest against tyranny. Plato's and Diogenes' practices of exposing pretentiousness and vanity as nonsensical grew out of a profound discontent with the violence of their era. Socrates and (probably) Plato were veterans of the Athenian army's disastrous war against Sparta. Socrates, Plato, and Diogenes distrusted the kind of confident public policies that drove Athens and its league of city-states into an almost suicidal struggle with Sparta and her allies. The Athenian war leadership under Pericles was proud, aristocratic, and driven by a quest for glory and control. Socrates and many of his fellow philosophers saw such a quest as utterly vain and—compared with an authentic search for the good, the true, and the beautiful—nonsensical. The Greco-Roman moralists did not use their philosophical tools to arrest all personal action or immobilize the human spirit (though some of the more radical skeptics in the ancient world, like Pyhrro, arguably came close to this end). In a phrase, they wanted to promote philosophical *development* rather than *growth*. Not all growth is good, and some (like the growth of a massive ego) can inhibit any further development or maturation. For Plato, Diogenes, and some of the other Greco-Roman moralists (Cicero, Dio Chrysostom, Seneca, Plutarch and others), the key to maturation was to retain a proper *eros* (Greek, meaning desire), which can also be interpreted as the retention of youth.

At the outset, three points need to be appreciated in locating Carroll in relation to this Greco-Roman background. First, Carroll was also at work during a time of imperial power and conflict. Although his works do not have the explicit political or moral content of ancient Platonic philosophy, Carroll wrote his work at the most prestigious and powerful university in the English-speaking world at the height of the British Empire. Carroll, like his Greco-Roman counterparts, can be read as exposing the dangers and, ultimately, the nonsense of pursuing worldly glory through power and manipulation. Second, for Socrates, Plato, Diogenes, and their fellow Greco-Roman moralists, *there was an appreciation of the goodness of human nature*. In different ways, Plato, Diogenes, Seneca, Cicero, and the other Greco-Roman moralists sought to expose as nonsense that which is or would become destructive to human life. In this matter, they have something in common with Lewis Carroll, who had a deep appreciation of the goodness, indeed the loveliness and sanity, of his child-heroine, Alice. Third, Carroll was very interested in both development and growth and the difference between these concepts.

The Nonsense of Lewis Carroll

Lewis Carroll pushes the boundaries of sense in *Alice in Wonderland* and *Through the Looking-Glass*, and yet he maintains a stable point of reference: Alice. Indeed, she is not perfect. For example, she doesn't notice the way that speaking of her cat should worry a mouse, and she betrays class consciousness in her reflections on whether she might be Mabel.

> I'm sure I can't be Mabel, for I know all sorts of things, and she, oh! she knows such a very little! . . .
>
> I must be Mabel after all, and I shall have to go and live in that poky little house, and have next to no toys to play with . . . No, I've made up my mind about it; if I'm Mabel, I'll stay down here![8]

But through all her adventures, Alice remains curious (and curiouser), sensible, and sane. She is the foil who exposes the nonsense in Carroll's worlds. Indeed she has to remain sane, polite, and sensible—otherwise she and we would not be able to appreciate the nonsense and follow Alice through the Rabbit-Hole World with abandon. While swimming in the pool of tears, for instance, Alice has this ultimately sensible exchange with a swimming mouse, who at first does not seem to understand her:

> "Perhaps it doesn't understand English," thought Alice; "I daresay it's a French mouse, come over with William the Conqueror." (For, with all her knowledge of history, Alice had no very clear notion how long ago anything had happened.) So she began again: "*Ou est ma chatte?*" which was the first sentence in her French lesson book.

The Mouse gave a sudden leap out of the water, and seemed to quiver all over with fright. "Oh, I beg your pardon!" cried Alice hastily, afraid that she had hurt the poor animal's feelings. "I quite forgot you didn't like cats."[9]

Chesterton got it half right when he used a rather bizarre analogy: "A blind man may be picturesque; but it requires two eyes to see the picture. And similarly even the wildest poetry of insanity can only be enjoyed by the sane."[10] While Chesterton was wrong about needing two eyes to see a picture (a cyclops could probably see well enough to cause mischief), he was onto something in his observation about insanity.

Alice must be sane for us to be carried along into the story, and so Carroll may be using nonsense to teach us a serious lesson about the value of nonsense and curiosity, and the dangers of pathos as it relates to the human tendency to control. Carroll uses nonsense to arouse curiosity in both Alice and the reader, and then he uses this curiosity as a critical component of sanity, acting as a check against excessive sympathy and empathy or, in short, pathos. Sympathy without pathos enables a certain distance, and encourages the reader to cede the desire to control the situation, to make it all better. In short, we enjoy the nonsense, dismiss any real danger, and go along with "what's next" rather than truly worrying about the possible demise of a little girl in an insane world.

Let's now consider what is insane about *Alice in Wonderland* (henceforth *AIW*) and *Through the Looking-Glass* (*TLG*).

Insanity in the Summer and Winter

There is quite a bit of nonsense in both of Carroll's famous books. As is often remarked, *AIW* is a summer book; it begins in the summer and has a comparatively more uplifting tone (truly a childhood adventure), whereas *TLG* is a winter book, darker in tone, mood (a somewhat nostalgic recollection of what was childhood), and plot. But throughout both books there are conversations that go nowhere, amazing misunderstandings, and cruel commands. Why is this amusing rather than horrifying? Because of Alice's sensibility, all the situations, characters, and commands are exposed as ludicrous and absurd. Consider Alice's response to the violently insane Queen:

> Alice began to feel very uneasy: to be sure, she had not as yet had any dispute with the Queen, but she knew that it might happen any minute, "and then," thought she, "what would become of me? They're dreadfully fond of beheading people here; the great wonder is, that there's any one left alive!"[11]

Not only do we see violent threats as impotent, but unintelligible insanity also becomes amusing:

> "Oh I know!" exclaimed Alice, who had not attended to [the] last remark. "[Mustard is] a vegetable. It doesn't look like one, but it is."
>
> "I quite agree with you," said the Duchess; "and the moral of that is—'Be what you would seem to be'—or, if you'd like it put more simply—'Never imagine yourself not to be otherwise than what it might appear to others that what you were or might have been was not otherwise than what you had been would have appeared to them to be otherwise.'"
>
> "I think I should understand that better," Alice said very politely, "if I had it written down: but I can't quite follow it as you say it."[12]

Readers are able to examine and experience *AIW*'s nonsensical situations without heart-pounding anxiety, pathos, or a desire to alter the action precisely because Alice is sensible, rational, and grounded. She does not panic or ever truly lament her predicament, which encourages the reader to disengage from the "normal" response of rejecting the Rabbit-Hole

World or identifying too closely with a lost little girl in a potentially dire situation.

Indeed, the world in which Alice finds herself is a very
dangerous world, with a great deal of death, negligence, and
uncertainty. Alice begins by not wanting to "kill anyone when
she falls"; there are thoughts about killing in the animal world
(for example, "Do cats eat bats?"); and chapter one of *AIW*
refers to "several nice little stories about children who had
got burnt, and eaten up by wild beasts and other unpleasant
things." Alice worries that she might shrink so much that she
becomes extinguished like a candle; the pool she creates is
from tears; and after a narrow escape she was "very glad to
find herself still in existence." Then there are the innumerable
charges and commands to execute various characters; when
Alice worries that she will be burned, she has to threaten to
unleash her cat in order to save herself. Alice is under constant
worries: she may be eaten by a dog, she may commit murder
when she contemplates abandoning a child, and so on.

All this would usually be enough to engender sympathy
and anxiety in the reader: a defenseless little girl in a dangerous universe at the mercy of tyrants, animals, and cruel situations. These are not the worries of a normal childhood, and
our response as readers, even in a Victorian time with a different construct of childhood, should be to worry about Alice,
sympathize with her, hope for her, and plan a way to control
the dangerous and insane world. Instead, Alice's very practical
approach—usually in some form of curiosity—propels us to follow her. Alice relays her predicaments and, through a narrative
voice, interprets them for the reader as more nonsensical than
harrowing. She herself says as much in "The Pool of Tears"
when she laments: "Oh dear, what nonsense I'm talking!"

Alice's situation is funny, in fact, because it is nonsense. Not
all nonsense is funny, of course (such as slavery in any era, including Diogenes', or other absurd and tragic situations), but Alice's
adventures in nonsense and absurdity remain firmly on the

amusing side of the balance sheet. They do not stray into the tragic or pathetic, partly because of Alice's character and response, partly because the potentially tragic outcomes never cross the line into actual tragedies.

The mixture of insanity and nonsense that is witnessed by a sane and sensible protagonist causes the reader—like Alice—to develop more of a curiosity about what is coming rather than a drive to understand everything that is happening. Often the need to understand something acts as a prelude to controlling it. In the Alice stories, however, curiosity, rather than control, is the condition for appreciating the humor inherent in Carroll's nonsense worlds.

From *Middlemarch*—certainly a novel without a lot of nonsense, but in the same era and mind-set as Carroll's work—we see an excellent example of this in Lydgate, the young doctor whose passion for medicine and need to understand the root causes of disease and pestilence are explicitly about controlling and changing a situation. There is no nonsense or humor in Lydgate's world to leaven his need to control or check things back to a "mere" curiosity. Clearly, the desire to eradicate pestilence and disease is an admirable passion, but, as illustrated in Lydgate's case, the excessive need to control everything eventually becomes a stumbling block toward ultimate success.

Curiosity's Double Edge

In addition to enabling an appreciation for nonsense and sanity, curiosity also leads Alice to a certain callousness that is frequently more apparent in children than adults. Consider, for example, the characters' offhand interactions with the baby pig or the kicking of Bill the lizard at the house; both examples are distinctly nonempathetic behavior, common in the Rabbit-Hole World. Without withdrawing the claim about the importance of Alice's basic goodness for the success of *AIW* and *TLG*, unbridled empathy and sympathy toward our child-heroine also cannot go unchecked for the two books to succeed humorously. Her curiosity and extraordinary adventures lead her into what might be called benign callousness, notwithstanding her politeness, etiquette, and efforts to help out some of her compatriots. Sometimes (or perhaps for much of the time), Alice is about "what's next"?

> "Hay, then," the King faintly murmured.
>
> Alice was glad to see that it revived him a good deal. "There's nothing like eating hay when you're faint," he remarked to [Alice], as he munched away.
>
> "I should think throwing cold water over you would be better," Alice suggested: "—or some sal-volatile."
>
> "I didn't say there was nothing *better*," the King replied. "I said there was nothing *like* it." Which Alice did not venture to deny.
>
> "Who did you pass on the road?" the King went on, holding out his hand to the Messenger for some more hay.
>
> "Nobody," said the Messenger.
>
> "Quite right," said the King: "this young lady saw him too. So of course Nobody walks slower than you."
>
> "I do my best," the Messenger said in a sullen tone. "I'm sure nobody walks much faster than I do!"[13]

Clearly, the focus remains on the absurd situations and not on the plight of a poor little girl caught in the midst of a battle.

A Curious Sanity and a Sane Curiosity?

As we've seen, Alice possesses some callousness, but also a goodness and sanity that make the unpredictable insanity of *AIW* and *TLG* delightfully nonsensical. Alice also displays some virtues that seem to mark adulthood or maturity, such as self-control, so noticeably absent in so many of the other characters. As W. H. Auden points out, Alice "is invariably self-controlled, and polite, while all the other inhabitants, human or animal, of Wonderland and the Looking-Glass are unsocial eccentrics—at the mercy of their passions and extremely bad-mannered, like the Queen of Hearts, the Duchess, the Hatter, and Humpty Dumpty, or grotesquely incompetent, like the White Queen and the White Knight."[14] But the self-control and sanity Alice displays are not so much, for Carroll, a matter of being an adult, as they are virtues essential to keeping the story going and having adventures. On this point, there is an interesting intersection between Plato and Lewis Carroll.

In Plato's *Republic*, the character Socrates begins the dialogue in a conversation with a venerable old man. The man has had a successful life, but now his passion for life has subsided. Socrates concludes that he cannot do philosophy with him. Instead, Socrates engages the younger men, who are filled with desire (*eros*) and questions about justice, the good, the arts, the role of women in an ideal society, and more. As Plato sees it, philosophy is a youthful activity. It is filled with *eros* and energy, curiosity, and a desire for serious investigation—not a pursuit for those who are old, tired, and have no questions. Connecting this theme with Carroll, the lament at the end of *TLG* suggests that when Alice grows up, she leaves the land of wonder, and thus the time for wonder. For Carroll and Plato, the point is not to leave the spirit of wonder, and thus not to leave that dimension of youth (perhaps even childhood) with its *eros* and energy. In this sense, Carroll, Plato, and the other Greco-Roman moralists endorse *development* (growing in wisdom, maturity, and virtues such as self-control) but not necessarily *growth* per se. There can be lots of growth that is not healthy; quite the opposite, as in the growth of a massive ego or the growth of despotic power.

An Objection

Consider briefly an objection to our strategy of relating Carroll with Plato, Diogenes, and other Greco-Roman moralists. The latter all had a fixed view of nature, which they took as a guiding reference point. For example, Diogenes Laertius writes "to be in accordance with Nature, that is, in accordance with the nature of man and that of the universe, doing nothing which the universal law is wont to forbid, that is, the right reason which pervades all things and is coextensive with Zeus."[15] Cicero makes a similar claim in *De Legibus*[16]: the nature of things is stable and divinely established. But in Carroll's universe, everything is topsy-turvy: there are talking animals, Alice can double in size or shrink as if by magic, she can fall almost endlessly and not be harmed, and so on. This seems a far cry from Diogenes' nature.

Our reply is that, actually, Carroll's insane world, with its girl-heroine getting bigger or smaller by drinking a potion, rabbits being able to tell time, and so on, highlights Carroll's command for the stability of morality itself. Tyrants (even when they are funny) are not rewarded for wanting to capriciously cut off heads, and at no time are we asked to imagine a topsy-turvy moral world in which it is good to be cruel, or in which respect and affection are treated as vices. Carroll thereby illustrates ways in which our specific duties might change under different, perhaps magical circumstances. If cats could engage in conversations with humans, presumably our moral duties to tell the truth would hold, though we don't have to worry about truth-telling or lying to creatures without language. On the stability of moral laws themselves, Carroll is at one with Diogenes, Cicero, Plato, and other Greco-Roman moralists.

A Nonsense Too Far?

Having argued that Carroll's work fits well into a broadly Socratic tradition that uses nonsense to help shape a moral personal identity, let us close by highlighting the problem of going too far with nonsense. There is an extensive literature of the absurd, highlighting absurd or nonsensical characters and institutions, developed by Franz Kafka, Nikolai Gogol, Eugene Ionesco, and others. Some of these works—like Kafka's *Metamorphosis* and *The Castle*—are definite classics. But as these works tread deeper and deeper into senseless strife and violence, especially in Kafka's unfinished novel, *The Trial*, life and death itself become almost meaningless.

And so here is our last claim: nonsense can be dangerous if you completely lose Alice or someone like Carroll's brave child-heroine, who maintains a sane goodness, accented perhaps with a tiny bit of benign callousness, and self-control amid all the absurdities to be found in life or fiction.[17] Indeed, if you fall into a Rabbit-Hole, here's hoping that you are with Alice!

NOTES

1. Cambridge, UK: Cambridge Scholars Publishing, 2008.
2. "Lewis Carroll" in *Forewords and Afterwords* (New York: Random House, 1973).
3. Tan Lin, "Introduction," in Lewis Carroll, *Alice's Adventures in Wonderland and Through the Looking-Glass* (New York: Barnes and Noble, 2004).
4. G. K. Chesterton, "The Library of the Nursery," in *Lunacy and Letters* (New York: Sheed & Ward, 1958), 26.
5. *Euthyphro* 14c3-4. *Plato's Euthyphro, Apology of Socrates and Crito*, ed. by John Burnet (Oxford: Clarendon Press, 2000)
6. *Republic* 587e2. Plato: Republic, intro. Charles M. Bakewell (New York: Charles Scribner's Sons, 1928), 328.
7. Diogenes Laertus, *Lives of Eminent Philosophers*, vol. II, trans. R. D. Hicks (London: William Heinemann, 1925), 31.
8. Carroll, *Alice's Adventures*, 25–26.
9. Ibid., 28–29.
10. G. K. Chesterton, *Orthodoxy* (New York: Barnes and Noble, 2007), 8.
11. Carroll, *Alice's Adventures*, 96.
12. Ibid., 105.
13. Carroll, *Through the Looking-Glass*, 228–229.

14. W. H. Auden, "Lewis Carroll," 289.
15. Diogenes Laertius, *Vitae Philosophorum* VII, 88, trans. H. S. Long (Oxonii: E Typographeo Clarendoniano, 1966), 104.
16. Cicero, *De Legibus* II, 4, 10. Cited in Alan Donagan, *The Theory of Morality* (Chicago: University of Chicago Press, 1977), 2.
17. We thank Jacob Zillhardt for comments.

"MEMORY AND MUCHNESS": ALICE AND THE PHILOSOPHY OF MEMORY

Tyler Shores

"I almost think I can remember feeling a little different. But if I'm not the same, the next question is, Who in the world am I? Ah, *that's* the great puzzle!"[1]

The need to know and the search for meaning are fundamental characteristics of children's literature and philosophical writings alike. So it's no surprise that *Alice's Adventures in Wonderland*, with its fantastical, nonsensical inversions, presents us with an ideal setting for philosophical reflection.

For instance, during her adventures through Wonderland, Alice encounters the Caterpillar, whose Socratic interrogation begins with a deceptively simple question:

"Who are *you*?" said the Caterpillar.
    This was not an encouraging opening for a conversation. Alice replied, rather shyly, "I—I hardly know, sir,

just at present—at least I know who I *was* when I got up this morning, but I think I must have been changed several times since then."[2]

Alice's conversation with the Caterpillar shows us how sometimes even the most complicated and important philosophical questions can lie just beneath a seemingly straightforward exchange. The ordinary question "Who are you?" leads Alice to confront one of the fundamental philosophical questions: "Who am I?" As the Caterpillar's cryptic responses begin to bewilder her more and more, Alice wonders at the Caterpillar's question, "So you think you're changed, do you?"

> "I'm afraid I am, sir," said Alice. "I can't remember things as I used" . . .
> "Can't remember *what* things?" said the Caterpillar.[3]

Alice cannot answer the question of who she is, because she can't seem to remember who she *was*. From this, we can begin to understand how memory is inextricably tied to questions of what we know (or perhaps think we know). Indeed, memory is crucially important for understanding ourselves as conscious, thinking individuals. But what *is* memory?

Memory is both familiar and mysterious. Sometimes it seems as if the things closest to us can be the hardest to understand—metaphors can be particularly helpful in such cases. Plato (427–347 BCE) likened memory to a wax tablet whose etchings were imprinted upon our souls. John Locke (1632–1704) envisioned memory as a type of storehouse for our ideas.

Perhaps a more helpful question to ask is: what does memory *mean* to us? Alice instinctively grasped the importance of memory to our sense of self. In helping us understand who we once were, memory helps us understand who we are now (and even who we will become). We make ourselves through our memories; after all, what we know is dependent on what we remember. On a deeper level, memory fulfills a desire we have to go back to the start, to understand where we have come from. Memory means so much to us because it holds the promise of permanence: "despite life's evanescent and transient qualities . . . memory [is] a resisting of time and mortality."[4]

For many philosophers, memory represents a way of knowing, a means to knowledge. In fact, for Plato, learning was simply another way of remembering the eternal truths that we already knew, but needed to relearn. In his dialogue *Meno*, Plato portrays Socrates as helping someone to "remember what he already knows without knowing that he knows,"[5] because we are all born with innate knowledge we are mostly unaware of until we're reminded of it. For the Greeks, memory was a gift from the Muses, a power to be invoked and bestowed upon the person hoping to perform some act of memory. As we'll see, the act of remembering becomes an important means of grasping a fuller knowledge of ourselves.

"Memory and Muchness"—Our Memory, Our Self

Alice ponders whether the changes she undergoes (first shrinking to a very tiny size and then growing to gigantic proportions) have changed who she is. In the process of her wondering, she stumbles upon the puzzle of personal identity and memory:

> Let me think: was I the same when I got up this morning? I almost think I can remember feeling a little different. But if I'm not the same, the next question is, Who in the world am I? Ah, *that's* the great puzzle![6]

Who are we? When we wake up each morning, we go about our daily lives with the assumption that we know who we are. To some extent our lives consist of our memories: we went here and there, did this and that, met him or her. When formulated in such a way, our memories are a crucial part of our self-identity. We are, in essence, the stuff of "memory and muchness,"[7] to borrow the drowsy words of the Dormouse. Our memories form the basis of who we are, and the accumulation of our past experience in turn determines our capacity to relate our past to our present. Alice's sense of self is shaken by this line of thinking, but a solution soon occurs to her: "I'll try if I know all the things I used to know."[8] This in turn raises another important question: are we the same person if we can remember who we were yesterday? Or five minutes ago? Conversely, are we a different person if we cannot remember what we thought we knew yesterday? The answers to these questions have significant implications for memory and its relation to self-identity. For one thing, who is that "I" when we say that "I remember" something? Part of the great puzzle that Alice has discovered is not just "Who am I?" but also the difference between the "I" of today, the "I" of yesterday, and the "I" of tomorrow.

This relation of memory and self is cleverly characterized in this dialogue from the French philosopher Denis Diderot (1713–1784):

> Diderot: Could you tell me what the existence of a sentient being means to that being himself?
>
> D'Alembert: Consciousness of having been himself from the first instant he reflected until the present moment.
>
> Diderot: But what is this consciousness founded on?
>
> D'Alembert: The memory of his own actions.
>
> Diderot: And without that memory?
>
> D'Alembert: Without that memory there would be no 'he,' because, if he only felt his existence at the moment

of receiving an impression, he would have no connected story of his life. His life would be a broken sequence of isolated sensations.

Diderot: All right. Now what is memory? Where does that come from?

D'Alembert: From something organic which waxes and wanes, and sometimes disappears altogether.[9]

Notice that Diderot talks about memory in relation to consciousness. For another philosopher of memory, John Locke, memory is a crucial part of his theory of the self. Memory for Locke is the means by which we can ensure continuity of consciousness and thus continuity of the self: "as far as any intelligent being can repeat the idea of any past action with the same consciousness it had of it at first, and with the same consciousness it has of any present action; so far is it the same personal self."[10] While we may not want to conclude that memory is the *only* means of defining our personal identity, Locke's emphasis on continuity and consciousness leads us to a still more important point, namely, that connectedness is an important part of our sense of self. Our sense of our past provides us with a meaningful context by which we can understand and relate to our present self.

Memory not only enables us to relate our past and present, but also serves to define our sense of self in relation to other selves (other people). This becomes a very important point of concern for Alice. If Alice cannot remember who she is, she assumes that she must be some other person:

I'm sure I can't be Mabel, for I know all sorts of things, and she, oh! she knows such a very little! Besides, *she's* she, and *I'm* I, and—oh dear, how puzzling it all is![11]

Like Alice, we have a need to understand our memory and, in turn, our own selves. Memory both shapes and is shaped by our sense of self. Memories are deeply personal, and in turn help define us as persons, because "memories are a highly subjective phenomenon (no one can remember what I remember)."[12] At the same time, it is important for us to remember that our memory of the past is really our *version* of the past, and not necessarily at all how things actually were.

During her encounter with the would-be philosopher Humpty Dumpty in *Through the Looking-Glass*, Alice is again reminded of this distinction between memory, self, and others. As with the Caterpillar, Alice's conversation with Humpty Dumpty proves vexing, although thoroughly philosophically interesting (at least for the reader):

> "Good-bye, till we meet again!" she said as cheerfully as she could.
>
> "I shouldn't know you again if we *did* meet," Humpty Dumpty replied in a discontented tone, giving her one of his fingers to shake; "you're so exactly like other people."[13]

On the surface, Humpty Dumpty's snub is his way of saying that Alice is rather boring and unmemorable. However, it's also worth noting that throughout her adventures in Wonderland and Looking-Glass country, Alice has a tendency to talk to herself in the second person: "for this curious child was very fond of pretending to be two people. 'But it's no use now,' thought Alice, 'to pretend to be two people!' Why, there's hardly enough of me left to make *one* respectable person!"[14] That split sense of self relates directly to another aspect of memory: "Memory first alienates us from ourselves in order to make it possible for us to reclaim ourselves."[15] According to St. Augustine (354–430), this is "where I bump up against myself, when I call back what I did, and where, and when, and how I felt when I was doing it."[16] There is something strange about the act of remembering, when we "bump up against" ourselves; we are in effect making our selves the object of our thinking. The philosophical implications of this type of self-scrutiny become evident as Augustine pursues this line of thinking further in wondering about the mind that thinks about itself: "Does it become its own twin, as it were, one staying here in order to do the viewing, the other moving there in order to be viewed, so it can be inside itself when seeing and in front of itself when seen?"[17] Alice's habit of thinking of herself as two different people in fact parallels that very same split sense of self that we experience during the act of memory.

Remembering to Forget

I'll try if I know all the things I used to know. Let me see: four times five is twelve, and four times six is thirteen, and four times seven is—oh dear![18]

—Alice

". . . and remember who you are!"[19]

—The White Queen to Alice

If memory is the basis of our understanding of our self, then what happens when we forget? When Alice resorts to mnemonics to test what she remembers in order to recover her sense of self, those memory devices ironically seem only to remind her of what she can't remember.

"[N]o, *that's* all wrong, I'm certain! I must have been changed for Mabel! I'll try and say '*How doth the little*' "—and she crossed her hands on her lap as if she were saying lessons, and began to repeat it, but her voice sounded hoarse and strange, and the words did not come the same as they used to do:—

"How doth the little crocodile
Improve his shining tail,
And pour the waters of the Nile

On every golden scale!

"How cheerfully he seems to grin,
How neatly spread his claws,
And welcome little fishes in
With gently smiling jaws!"

"I'm sure those are not the right words," said poor
Alice, and her eyes filled with tears again as she went
on, "I must be Mabel after all."[20]

Note the mechanical, ritualized way in which Alice prepares
to recite her rhymes. This type of memory was particularly
of interest to the philosopher Henri Bergson (1859–1941),
who believed there were two forms of memory: memories of
habit ("remembering how") and memories of personal events
("remembering when"). According to Bergson, "once a lesson is mastered (and becomes a habit) it becomes impersonal;
I just go ahead and repeat it without thinking of it as something
that is part of my life in particular. Anyone else might have
learned this material."[21] Alice goes about things in a different
way; she tries to use her impersonal knowledge as the means to
remembering her personal sense of self. Bergson's advice
to Alice would be to try and remember the personal details
that accompanied her memory of "How doth the little . . ."
The lesson from Alice's forgetfulness is that the past may be
remembered (or misremembered) in many ways.

If we cannot remember who we are, then who are we? In
the forest-with-no-names Alice finds herself confronted with
an existential crisis when she cannot remember her own name:
"And now, who am I? I *will* remember, if I can! I'm determined to
do it!"[22] Alice's inability to remember her own name is tied to a
greater issue of personal identity; as her question implies, it
isn't simply her name she can't remember, but *who* she is. Yet
at the same time, the fact that we still can remember that we
are forgetting something means that we are not totally forgetting. As the philosopher Martin Heidegger (1889–1976) notes,

"Complete forgetting . . . is forgetting the forgetting, disappearance of the very disappearance, where the covering over is itself covered over."[23]

The great German philosopher Friedrich Nietzsche (1844–1900) wrote about this very subject in one of his earliest works, *Untimely Meditations*. Nietzsche draws on two examples in illustrating his thoughts on forgetting: that of the animal (cattle "do not know what is meant by yesterday or today"[24]) and the young child (who "plays in blissful blindness between the hedges of past and future"[25]). Coincidentally, a young child and an animal just so happen to be what we find when Alice and her companion the Fawn wander about the forest of forgetting. In his meditations on forgetting, Nietzsche suggests that we need to strive for a balance that enables us to have the right perspective toward our past and present, and subsequently our future as well. This leads us to wonder about our own natural assumptions. Is forgetting always such a bad thing? For better or for worse, we all carry memories that we wish we could remember more, as well as memories that we wish we could remember less. Nietzsche states that "it is altogether impossible to *live* at all without forgetting."[26] In *Through the Looking-Glass*, the chess-piece-size King exclaims his shock at being lifted in the air by the normal-size Alice: "the horror of that moment! I shall never ever forget!"[27] From this, we might consider that sometimes there are instances in which forgetting is more of a virtue to us than remembering, and thus "[i]t is critically important that human happiness requires both the capacity to forget and the capacity to remember, because human beings cannot live without forgetting any more than they can live without remembering."[28]

Lewis Carroll, mindful of the fleetingness of childhood, opens his second Alice book with a poem that is notably elegiac in tone. Since childhood is destined to become only a thing of memory, and that memory, too, is something that inevitably, inexorably fades, Carroll writes of thoughts, "Whose echoes live in memory yet, / Though envious years would say 'forget.'"[29] Forgetting is in many ways an ironic reminder of how much value remembering has for us.

Memory, Dreams, and Imagination:
"Curiouser and Curiouser!"

Forgetting is an instance of what Sigmund Freud (1856–1939) called "alienated memory": memory that is both a part of us, but somehow separate from our everyday conscious experiences. Freud is especially relevant to our exploration of memory, as dreams are a significant aspect of Alice's adventures. We do not always remember our dreams, and in this way, "dreams constituted another example of alienated memory, because their content might be wholly or partially unavailable after waking, while conversely, things might be remembered in dreams that had long been forgotten in waking life."[30] And of course, Alice's dreams are the point of entry in both her adventures into Wonderland and through Looking-Glass country.

Dreams take on an existentially relevant importance for Alice. While encountering the twins Tweedledum and Tweedledee, Alice notices the Red King sleeping under a tree, at which point Tweedledee says that the King must be dreaming of Alice and poses the question:

> "And if he left off dreaming about you, where do you suppose you'd be?"
>
> . . . "You'd be nowhere. Why, you're only a sort of thing in his dream!"
>
> "If that there King was to wake," added Tweedledum, "you'd go out—bang!—just like a candle!"
>
> "I shouldn't!" Alice exclaimed indignantly. "Besides, if *I'm* only a sort of thing in his dream, what are *you*, I should like to know?" . . .

"Well, it's no use *your* talking about waking him," said Tweedledum, "when you're only one of the things in his dream. You know very well you're not real."

"I *am* real!" said Alice, and began to cry.

"You won't make yourself a bit realer by crying," Tweedledee remarked: "there's nothing to cry about."

"If I wasn't real," Alice said—half laughing through her tears, it all seemed so ridiculous—"I shouldn't be able to cry."

"I hope you don't suppose those are real tears?" Tweedledum interrupted in a tone of great contempt.[31]

Alice becomes increasingly upset at the troubling thought that she may be nothing more than a thing in someone else's imagination. In the worlds that Lewis Carroll has conjured up from his own imagination, the line between memory, dreams, and imagination is decidedly blurred. When is remembering actually remembering, and not simply imagining that we remember? Imagination may in some ways serve to fill the gaps of our memory; but intentionally or otherwise, "imagination very often presents us with a past that we wish we had lived, or with the past as we now wish we had lived."[32] Just as Freud stressed the interpretative aspect of our dreams, our imagination and memory require a similar act of interpretation on our parts. Memory can present us with a possible meaning, but that meaning still must be interpreted. In interpreting the memories of our past, we are at the same time retrieving a sense of our self from that past and fashioning our current selves in the present.

At the end of *Through the Looking-Glass* (the last chapter is entitled, "Which Dreamed It?"), Alice muses: "Let's consider who it was that dreamed it all. This is a serious question . . . it *must* have been either me or the Red King. He was part of my dream, of course—but then I was part of his dream, too! *Was* it the Red King?"[33] The book offers no suggestion of an answer, only an invitation for all of us to consider that tricky relation-ship between dreams, imagination, and memory: "Which do you think it was?"[34] In this way, we're all invited to remember that the relationship between imagination and memory must be constantly held to interpretation—that just as we wonder what our dreams mean, we should wonder the same with regard to our memories.

From Backwards-Working Memory, or Working Backwards from Memory?

The backwardness of Lewis Carroll's fictional worlds leads us to questions that seem out of place in our everyday thinking. For instance, what if our memories ran in the opposite direc-tion? As Alice encounters the White Queen, her puzzlement is increased when learning about how backwards-seeming everything is:

> "Living backwards!" Alice repeated in great astonish-ment. "I never heard of such a thing!"
>
> "—but there's one great advantage in it, that one's memory works both ways."
>
> "I'm sure *mine* only works one way," Alice remarked. "I can't remember things before they happen."
>
> "It's a poor sort of memory that only works back-wards," the Queen remarked.[35]

What would a world be like in which we remembered things that had yet to happen? If such were the case, we might ask ourselves which we valued more: the experience, or the memory of the experience? Or to invert the question—what is an experience to us without the memory of it afterward? Memory of an experience needs a context in order to be mean-ingful to us—and in this way, experience may be thought of as a continuous process of contextualizing, like "a set of Chinese boxes, one fitting perfectly inside or around another."[36]

This inversion of how we normally understand memory leads us to another important aspect of memory, its inherently temporal quality. Memory is the defining way in which we relate to our own past; it is the meeting point of our past and our present, and that which guides our outlook toward the future. According to Augustine, memory is the common tie between these different divisions of time: "We cannot properly say that the future or past exists, or that there are three times, past, present, and future."[37] Augustine suggests that it is through memory that we may glimpse an understanding of time that is one and the same: "the present of the past, the present of the present, and the present of the future."[38] Carroll similarly combines this sense of past and future selves, in poetically noting that "we are but older children."[39] The question then becomes, what is the relation between our past self and our present self? Our memory, as Locke observed, is dependent upon our sense of time and self. Think for instance of Alice's confusion when she isn't sure she can remember who she is from one minute (past) to the next (present, future): "How puzzling all these changes are! I'm never sure what I'm going to be, from one minute to another!"[40] Poor Alice! She is left disoriented and can only help but wonder: if she was different from who she was before, who is she now? While the past is very much a part of our lives, life itself is an ongoing process, and thus the question of what the past means to us must always be an open one. The past is by definition that which is finished and gone and it is always being added to, as our present becomes the past. Our past and our present are set in a mutually defining relationship—we respond to the past, and the past in turn affects us.

Alice perfectly draws together the themes of memory, time, and self when she remarks, "I'd nearly forgotten that I've got to grow up again!"[41] In this instance, Alice is referring to the fact that she was very tiny, but the other meaning—that she will have to become an adult—is very telling. Memory becomes a working metaphor for Wonderland. In both Wonderland and in our memories there resides an unspoken desire for things not to change, for us to forget to grow up again. Alice, when stuck in the White Rabbit's house, notes: "And when I grow up . . . but I'm grown up now," she added in a sorrowful tone; "at least there's no room to grow up any more *here*."[42]

Memory relates us to our past, informs our relation to the present, and determines our attitudes toward our future. Perhaps there is a healthy balance to be found between remembering and forgetting, and Alice clearly has the right idea in saying, "But it's no use going back to yesterday, because I was a different person then."[43] We live in memory, and by memory, but as Alice tells us, we needn't be troubled by the thought that the person we remember being yesterday may be different from the person we are now, or are yet to become.

NOTES

1. Lewis Carroll, *The Philosopher's Alice: Alice's Adventures in Wonderland and Through the Looking-Glass*. Introduction and notes by Peter Heath (New York: St. Martin's Press, 1974), 24. All subsequent references to the *Alice* stories are from this text.
2. Ibid., 47.
3. Ibid., 48.
4. Evelyne Ender, *Architexts of Memory: Literature, Science, and Autobiography* (Ann Arbor: University of Michigan Press, 2005), 179.
5. Kurt Danziger, *Marking the Mind: A History of Memory* (Cambridge, UK: Cambridge University Press, 2008), 93
6. Carroll, *The Philosopher's Alice*, 24.
7. Ibid., 74.
8. Ibid., 24.
9. Denis Diderot, *Rameau's Nephew and D'Alembert's Dream*, trans. Leonard Tancock (New York: Penguin, 1976), 155.
10. John Locke, *An Essay Concerning Human Understanding* (New York: Dover, 1959), vol. 1, 451.
11. Carroll, *The Philosopher's Alice*, 24.
12. Ender, *Architexts of Memory*, 12.
13. Carroll, *The Philosopher's Alice*, 198.

14. Ibid., 20.
15. Cited in Garry Wills, *Saint Augustine's Memory* (New York: Viking, 2002), 12.
16. Saint Augustine, *Confessions*, trans. Garry Wills (New York: Penguin, 2006), 219.
17. Saint Augustine, *The Trinity*. Book 14, Paragraph 8, in Wills, *Saint Augustine's Memory*, 12.
18. Carroll, *The Philosopher's Alice*, 24.
19. Ibid., 150.
20. Ibid., 24–25.
21. Danziger, *Marking the Mind*, 165.
22. Carroll, *The Philosopher's Alice*, 159.
23. Cited in Jean-Louis Chrétien, *The Unforgettable and the Unhoped For* (New York: Fordham University Press, 2002), 2.
24. Friedrich Nietzsche, *Untimely Meditations* (Cambridge, UK: Cambridge University Press, 1983), 60.
25. Ibid., 61.
26. Ibid., 62.
27. Carroll, *The Philosopher's Alice*, 159.
28. Jeffrey Blustein, *The Moral Demands of Memory* (Cambridge, UK: Cambridge University Press, 2008), 7.
29. Carroll, *The Philosopher's Alice*, 124.
30. Danziger, *Marking the Mind*, 106.
31. Carroll, *The Philosopher's Alice*, 169–170.
32. Anthony Paul Kerby, *Narrative and the Self* (Bloomington: Indiana University Press, 1991), 25.
33. Carroll, *The Philosopher's Alice*, 241.
34. Ibid.
35. Ibid., 177.
36. Kerby, *Narrative and the Self*, 16.
37. Augustine, *Confessions*, 271.
38. Ibid.
39. Carroll, *The Philosopher's Alice*, 124.
40. Ibid., 55.
41. Ibid., 45.
42. Ibid., 40.
43. Ibid., 100.

CONTRIBUTORS

Pawns and Pieces: As Arranged before
Commencement of Game

Robert Arp developed an interest in informatics ontology, philosophy of biology, and the philosophy of popular culture after foolishly consuming the contents of a bottle labeled DRINK ME at his first college pub night. For years thereafter—and until a recent intervention by his colleagues—his scholarly articles all mysteriously began, "Twas brillig, and the slithy toves did gyre and gimble in the wabe." Arp is founder, past-president, and thirty-third-degree member of the Jabberwocky Society of America.

David S. Brown is associate professor and Chair of the Department of Philosophy at Lindenwood University. He is currently planning a sabbatical to find the right rabbit-hole and, using nothing except Occam's razor, digging his way to Wonderland—where, if his funding comes through, he will take a group of insane mathematicians to play billiards. He is currently in therapy for an obsession to tip Humpty off the wall onto Richard Dawkins, and then eating tarts over the remains while shouting "Glory!" He sometimes sees Nobody when he's not looking.

Richard Brian Davis is associate professor of philosophy at Tyndale University College. He also teaches philosophy at Glendon College, York University (Toronto, Canada). His publications include articles in *X-Men and Philosophy* and *24 and Philosophy*, which he co-edited with Jennifer Hart Weed and Ronald Weed (Wiley, 2007). Davis recently discovered that if you take Morpheus's red and blue pills *together*, you can wake up in Wonderland *and* believe whatever you want to believe—all while lying in bed. Does it get any better than that?

George A. Dunn regularly co-teaches a course called "Philosophy through Pop Culture" at Purdue University at Indianapolis. A recognized expert on cylons, vampires, and mutants, Dunn's articles have appeared in *Terminator and Philosophy* and *Twilight and Philosophy*. His magnum opus and life's work, "Arithmetic, Ambition, Distraction, Uglification, and Derision," has recently been accepted for publication with the prestigious Mock Turtle University Press.

Ron Hirschbein's misadventures in Nuclear Wonderland began as visiting professorships at several institutes at University of California campuses in San Diego and Berkeley, where his research focused upon postmodern approaches to nuclear crises (he never met a meta-narrative he didn't like). He went on to create programs in war and peace studies at California State University, Chico, where he's semi-retired. Once when participating in the University of New Mexico's magical mystery tour of U.S. atomic facilities, he recklessly announced, "But I don't want to go among mad people." His punishment? The forced consumption of New Mexican green chilies while absorbing residual radiation at the Trinity atomic test site. This may transform him into a mutant suitable for the next Pop Culture volume.

Dennis Knepp teaches philosophy and religious studies at Big Bend Community College in Moses Lake, Washington—which may have begun as a pool of tears, though it scarcely contains a talking mouse, let alone one that came over with William the Conqueror. Knepp's "Bella's Vampire Semiotics" appears in *Twilight and Philosophy*. Do drop by his office when you're in town to talk about Alice, mice, or vampires. But a word to the wise. Don't mention *cats*: "nasty, low, vulgar things!"

Megan S. Lloyd is a professor of English at King's College in Wilkes-Barre, Pennsylvania, and the author of *"Speak It in Welsh": Wales and the Welsh Language in Shakespeare* as well as articles on Shakespeare and performance, medieval drama, and the Welsh in Renaissance England. While Megan and the White Rabbit have a lot in common, she would rather be like the White Queen and live backwards.

Brian McDonald is a senior lecturer in literature at Indiana University–Purdue University Indianapolis where he specializes in the teaching of the classics and the development of online courses. An early love of the Alice books has prepared him admirably for life in the academy. Not only has the computer side of his work given him a new appreciation for the logic of Wonderland, but Alice's experiences have taught him how to avoid extended debates with those of his colleagues who are lineal descendants of Humpty Dumpty. Yesterday, he managed to believe four impossible things before breakfast, but fell short of the White Queen's record when he couldn't see himself as the square root of 16. Very few people can these days, you know.

Rick Mayock has always loved adventures (reading about them, that is) and explanations (but as the Gryphon says "adventures first!"). He teaches philosophy at West Los Angeles College, and has contributed to *The Beatles and Philosophy* and *The Office and Philosophy*. He is even fonder of riddles that have no answers and, like Lewis Carroll, is a fan of really bad puns. His students say they are not sure of the porpoise of his philosophy classes, but at least, they say, he tortoise well.

Elizabeth Olson received her BA degree in English and philosophy from Oberlin College and her MBA from the Wharton School. She writes, reads, plays the cello, and raises two small children with her spouse in Minneapolis. Liz hopes to publish her novel at some point in the future, but for now, her day job is as chief financial officer of a consulting firm with offices in Minneapolis, Washington, D.C., and New York. Her own experience suggests that the corporate world is very much a Wonderland, and depending on the day, Liz worries that she has adopted the role of the Queen of Hearts—or even the Duchess.

Scott F. Parker lives in Minnesota, where everything is large, especially the mushrooms and blue caterpillars. Parker has published widely on pop culture and philosophy, including essays on *Lost*, football, the iPod, and golf. Neighbors complained recently when he took down his satellite dish and replaced it with a long smoking hookah. Alas, Parker takes not the smallest notice of them or of anything else.

Brendan Shea is a PhD candidate at the University of Illinois and is currently working on a dissertation in the philosophy of science. He has also contributed an essay to *Twilight and Philosophy*. His research for the essay in this volume included numerous trips to Wonderland. While there, he mistakenly showed a copy of his essay to the Queen of Hearts, who promptly had him arrested for "confessing to taking a tart." Humpty Dumpty, the appointed public defender, has advised him not to say any more.

Tyler Shores is a graduate student in English at University of Oxford. He received his BA in English and Rhetoric from University of California, Berkeley, where he created and for six semesters taught a course called "The Simpsons and Philosophy" (inspired by William Irwin's book of the same name). Tyler has also contributed to *Heroes and Philosophy*. He spends much of his free time forgetting about things he's supposed to remember (or was that remembering things he's supposed to forget?), and wandering about Christ Church—where Lewis Carroll wrote *Alice's Adventures in Wonderland*. He swears he's seen a White Rabbit rushing off to somewhere.

Charles Taliaferro, professor of philosophy, St. Olaf College, is the author or editor of eleven books, including *Evidence and Faith* (Cambridge University Press, 2005), and he has contributed to philosophy and popular culture books on *Lost*, superheroes, Narnia, and other topics. He looks like a large Rabbit and is constantly looking at his watch and saying, "Oh dear! Oh dear! I shall be too late!"

Mark W. Westmoreland teaches Philosophy at Penn State–Brandywine and Neumann College. His research interests include continental philosophy, race theory, and philosophy of history and culture. Like Alice, Mark often feels as if he is falling down the rabbit hole. Although he never knows what day it is, he always has the time. No matter what task lies before him, Mark always makes room for a little daydream filled with adventure.

Mark D. White is a professor in the Department of Political Science, Economics, and Philosophy at the College of Staten Island/CUNY, where he teaches courses combining economics, philosophy, and law. His edited books include *Iron Man and Philosophy: Facing the Stark Reality* (Wiley, 2010), *The Thief of Time: Philosophical Essays on Procrastination* (with Chrisoula Andreou; Oxford, 2010), *Watchmen and Philosophy* (Wiley, 2009), *Theoretical Foundations of Law and Economics* (Cambridge, 2009), and *Batman and Philosophy* (with Robert Arp; Wiley, 2008). He is currently writing a book collecting and expanding upon his work on economics and Kantian ethics, but "it's very hard with that silly Cat grinning at me all the time."

Daniel Whiting is lecturer in philosophy at the University of Southampton. His principal areas of research are philosophy of language and philosophy of mind, and he's published a number of articles in international journals, as well as the edited collection *The Later Wittgenstein on Language* (Palgrave, 2009). Taking his lead from Tweedledee (or was it Tweedledum?), Whiting has managed to convince his students that it's no use *their* talking to him about their grades, when they're only things in his dream. Crying won't help, either. For you don't suppose those are *real* tears, do you?

INDEX

"Down, Down, Down": What You Will Find at the Bottom